When God Says Wait

finding joy in the journey

by
Shelly Divido

For more information or to connect with our ministry, visit
www.lightoftheworldjax.org

Table of Contents

Summer

Autumn

Winter

Spring

DEDICATIONS

To my daughter, Hannah Grace, who has taught me to find joy in every moment and every season of life. You have introduced the beauty of grace upon grace to me through every trial and victory. You are my greatest gift. May you always know the deep, steadfast love of Jesus.

To my husband Harry, who has fought beside me through the waiting every step of the way. I'm thankful for every (yes, *every*) sacrifice and every act of faith that you have made. I'm so thankful to be on this lifelong adventure with you.

AUTHOR'S NOTES

My name is Shelly Divido. I was adopted as a newborn baby and raised in Butler, Pennsylvania. I grew up in in an Evangelical church and met Jesus when I was just a little girl.

Ever since I was small, my heart longed to serve people. After a two-week mission trip to Uganda, I knew that the missionary life was calling my name. This love of missions led my husband and I to start Light of the World Ministries, a non-profit organization based in Jacksonville, Florida in 2011. It serves what we refer to as the least of these. Our ministry was started by handing out peanut butter and jelly sandwiches and water to homeless people.

Over the years we've served homeless men and woman, families in low-income housing, hosted food distributions and international mission trips to Central America. We've partnered with many different churches, organizations, and individuals to take the name of Jesus to the ends of the earth.

In 2016, our ministry bought some land in Central America where we continue to build a Rescue Center for orphans, widows, and families in need. In

2018, we moved there to begin building a safe place where those in need can come to receive food, help with schooling, temporary housing and most importantly, encounter Jesus.

As we stepped out in faith the Lord brought one very special little girl into our family, one with a story that was very similar to mine. Adoption has always been close to my heart and only God could build our family with two stories so intertwined.

On August 11, 2015, the Lord had placed a little girl named Hannah Grace on my heart. I didn't know where she was, if she was born yet, or when I would meet her. I didn't know how I would become her mother, but my heart felt like being her mother was just a part of who I was created to be, so I prayed. The Lord gave me the name Hannah Grace. Hannah means favor or grace of God. Her name means grace upon grace, as in John 1:16. *"From His fullness we receive grace upon grace."* I prayed for her by name for years and often struggled, wondering if I had heard Him correctly. The waiting seemed almost unbearable as I longed to hold that little girl in my arms.

In November 2017, we said goodbye to our home in Jacksonville, only leaving with a few suitcases as we began our journey to Central America to serve and build the Rescue Center. We thought this was going to be a short, three-month trip, but along the way we got the call that Hannah Grace was about to enter our family. Her birth mother was from a family that we considered to be our own family. We had "adopted" them through another ministry and had been helping with food and schooling. We celebrated life's greatest joys and life's hardest trials together. We shared life with them. She is a single mother of seven children and was left unable to care for another beautiful baby. Her greatest loss and sacrifice of love has been my greatest gift as she surrendered her rights so that I could be called mom.

Our mission for the Rescue Center has always been to build it up and then equip the right people to run it. We have never felt called to live abroad long term. We have been believing God for the impossible as the paperwork, red tape, and issues between the two countries has left us unable to return to our home country together as a family. Through it all I knew from the beginning that she was my baby. Just as I waited for the Lord to place her in my hands, I continue waiting to watch the miracle unfold. One day we will return to our home, but for now God says, "wait".

Introduction
When God Says Wait

This book has been birthed out of my own, long and personal journey through the wilderness. As we dive in together over the next forty days my prayer is that you would be strengthened in the Lord and encouraged to wait well. When God told me to wait, my human nature fought it almost every step of the way. For a long time, I tried to keep my life aligned with my own definition of "normal" even though the Lord asked me to lay it all down and wait. Then, I surrendered to the season He had placed me in. It was only after my surrender that I could begin walking with Him through the process of waiting. This book is an offering to the Lord. It is an act of laying my life down. I pray that you would experience the joy that I have found through the adventure of walking with Jesus through every season.

When I walked into my season of waiting, I felt like my life had just fallen apart. My identity had been so wrapped up in staying busy and being productive that when things got quiet, my heart freaked out. All the things that my heart needed to deal with came rushing to the surface, overflowing out of my heart. I'd been suppressing and avoiding all of it. There was so much that needed to be healed inside of me. There were also many things inside of me that I didn't even realize were there. There are many processes involved in waiting. It tends to strip us of the worldly identity that we have built for ourselves along the way. It is in the stripping, when we are all alone with Jesus in the wilderness, that we find everything our heart desires.

There are many different scenarios that can lead us into a season of waiting. God may simply ask you to lay down your life and follow Him. You may be waiting for a baby. You may be in transition. You may have made poor decisions. You may have lost a loved one. You may have also been obediently following God's voice to do what He's called you to do. However, you started your journey, I pray that you are encouraged by the words in this book. I pray that, while things may be stripped away from your heart, the foundation that is established during your time in the wilderness releases you into freedom, joy and into the heart of the Father. I pray that you experience God's heart in a new way. I pray that you grow deeply and abundantly into all God has for you these next forty days.

Waiting has purpose. Though the days seem long, and your heart may feel weary you can rest in knowing that God will meet you right where you are. He will meet you in your questions. He will meet you in your brokenness, your grief, your anger. He will meet you in the silence. I encourage you to set aside the next 40 days to do nothing more than meet with Him. May you be filled to overflowing as you experience the goodness

and kindness of God during your beautiful season of
waiting.

Summer

Wait for the LORD;
be strong and courageous.
Wait for the LORD.
Psalms 27:14 HCSB

Day One
The Wait Begins

So it went on year by year. As often as she went up to the house of the LORD, she used to provoke her. Therefore Hannah wept and would not eat. 'Hannah, why do you weep? And why do you not eat? And why is your heart sad? Am I not more to you than ten sons?'
1 Samuel 1:7-8 ESV

The Merriam Webster Dictionary defines the word wilderness as *"a tract or region uncultivated and uninhabited by human beings."* It makes sense why people describe unknown and isolated seasons as a wilderness. It's difficult to know what to do when we are thrust into situations that leave our life in chaos and uncertainty, yet it happens to all of us at one time or another. Things happen in life. Maybe you have lost a loved one. Maybe you have lost a job. Maybe you experienced a car accident. Maybe the entire world goes through a pandemic. Every day we experience things that are outside our control. Those situations can leave us gasping for air. They can leave us searching for anything that we can control. They leave us wanting to cling to anything that feels comfortable and familiar.

Those same situations give us a choice. The choice to run to God or the choice to get angry and blame Him for what is going on around us. Sometimes, we make that choice, based on how quickly we see God respond to our cry for help. Oftentimes, we see an immediate response to the prayers we've prayed, leaving everything right in our world once again. Other times the prayers we pray seem to go unanswered. And so, the wait begins.

Many times, throughout a given day there are things within our control that we can decide to wait for or act on. The dishes need to be washed. The bills need to be paid. The dog needs to be walked. These things flow within our normal schedules and rhythms of life, but there are also many things that are completely outside our control that cause us to wait. These things are usually categorized in the "needing a miracle" section of life. Infertility, a cancer diagnoses, a financial crisis, a paperwork nightmare and the list goes on and on. You name it and someone is going through it. They have entered the waiting zone. The thing about waiting is, it usually comes suddenly. One night you go to bed and your life is normal. The next morning you wake up and everything has changed. There is nothing that can prepare you to suddenly be waiting, but there you are, waiting for a miracle.

It reminds me of Hannah in I Samuel chapter 1. She longed for a child, but the LORD had 'closed her womb'. It doesn't say why her womb was closed, but the Bible does tell us that this went on for years and years. She was tormented. She was depressed. She even became bitter. She felt all the feelings we go through when we wake up one day and realize our normal is no longer normal. Hannah was forced into waiting. She became desperate for God through her waiting as she knew that He was the only One that could heal her womb. People even judged her as they couldn't understand what she was going through, but Hannah continued to seek God with all her heart. She had a choice to be angry with God or worship Him.

She chose to press in, to lay her life down, and worship God. Even through her struggles she believed that God was who He said He was. The God of Abraham, Isaac, and Jacob.

They rose early in the morning and worshiped before the LORD; then they went back to their house at Ramah. And Elkanah knew Hannah his wife, and the LORD remembered her. And in due time Hannah conceived and bore a son, and she called his name Samuel, for she said, "I have asked for him from the LORD. 1 Samuel 1:19-20 ESV

The Bible doesn't tell us how many years Hannah faced infertility, but it does say that it was years. She faced every emotion you could imagine, yet she chose to wait on God. She chose to surrender her heart and worship through the darkest nights. From there, God honored her faith and remembered her. He remembered her. He remembered her tears. He remembered all her prayers. He remembered her faithfulness and in due time, Hannah had a son. Her miracle was no longer in waiting but held securely in her arms.

I don't know how long you've been waiting. Maybe you have just gotten news that you are in desperate need of a miracle. Or perhaps you have been waiting a while and just need some encouragement. Today I want you to know that you have a choice. You can choose to walk through this season with complete surrender and trust knowing that God is going to use this time for your good and His glory, or you can sit and wallow and be angry because of your circumstances. The choice is yours. Will you choose to be like Hannah and worship through this time? One thing I know for sure is that God sees you and He will remember you. There is a process in your season of waiting. Will you walk with Him on this journey through the wilderness? God wants to use this time to perfect His love in you. As you go through your day, dig into the story of Hannah in 1 Samuel 1 and 2. Be encouraged that this is not the end. It is simply the start of something new.

Day Two
The Joy Of Waiting

*Count it all joy, my brothers, when you meet trials
of various kinds, for you know that the testing of
your faith produces steadfastness. And let
steadfastness have its full effect that you may
be perfect and complete, lacking in nothing.
James 1:2-4 ESV*

I don't know about you but waiting never used to
produce joy in me. The amount of hatred I had for
waiting even took the joy out of surprises. Any time I
would give a gift or receive I gift I wanted to do it now. I
didn't want to wait till the celebration. So much so that
one time I saved up money to give my husband a small
shopping spree to his favorite store for his birthday. I
bought the gift card two weeks in advance, and I could
not wait to give it to him. I don't remember exactly, but I
might have waited a week before I caved and gave it to
him. It wasn't even that he begged for it early, it was
simply my inability to wait. And while my husband did
love the gift, there was nothing waiting for him on his
birthday. We have never been big on giving gifts, but I
just think back to how much sweeter that gift would

have been if I had waited to give it when the time was right.

You might be thinking, "What in the world does this have to do with my waiting?" My point is that it is possible to wait well. Your waiting might be produced by circumstances completely outside your control. It may have caused deep anger, depression, bitterness, or grief. You may not see a way out or another side to those emotions right now, but the thoughts you are having and the way you feel will one day end. While it is important to process those emotions, they were not meant to stay with you forever. God's heart is for you to be complete and lacking nothing. That is why it says in James 1:2 to *count our trials as joy.* It is because the trials are for our benefit. What God does in our hearts during times of waiting produces pure gold. It brings everything inside of us out so that God can realign and reshape our hearts to produce steadfastness, perseverance, and endurance.

God is more concerned about your heart than your circumstances when He leads you to wait. It's the process in between the trial and the promise land where He does the best work. Why, you ask? Because it's in that process that He's molding you into the person He created you to be. Unlike my hatred for waiting, God loves when you wait on Him. My timing wasn't perfect when I gave my husband his birthday present. Yet, God's timing is always perfect. He is always steadfast and patient. It's just who He is. He is not in a rush to fix everything that looks broken to you, because

He sees the big picture. He knew you before you were born. He knows the day you will take your last breath on earth. He knows every day in between. Part of waiting on the Lord removes our strength so that our weakness can glorify Him.

Your time of waiting is not meant to be miserable. It is not meant to leave you broken. This time will heal you, restore you, and increase you if you will let it. You may not be able to see that right now. You may feel like your heart has been shattered, but I need you to know that you are loved. You are held in the hands of your Heavenly Father. You may not feel Him right now. You may still be angry with Him. Yet, it does not change that He is with you, always. His timing is perfect. Will you sit with Him today? Regardless of how you feel, will you let Him lavish His love on you? You can receive His joy today. You can make a decision to wait well. He is working on your heart in ways you never could imagine and all He needs is for you to rest in Him and count all your trials as joy. You may not see it today, but these trials are leading to joy. They are being used for your good and for His glory. Today I encourage you to choose to hope again. Psalms 27:13-14 says,

"I am certain that I will see the LORD's goodness in the land of the living. Wait for the LORD; be strong and courageous. Wait for the LORD." HCSB

His timing is perfect. He is faithful and true. Seek Him today. God is releasing joy into your waiting today.

Day Three
Boundaries Rediscovered

*"Sarai said to Abram, "Since the LORD has
prevented me from bearing children, go to my
slave; perhaps through her I can build a family."
And Abram agreed to what Sarai said."*
Genesis 16:2 HCSB

Boundaries are something we all have whether
we realize it or not. Some of us protect those boundaries
while others have no idea what boundaries really are.
Regardless, we all have them. We actually have
boundaries all throughout life that we rarely give notice
to. Your property has boundaries. The grocery store has
boundaries. Your children have boundaries. There are
just certain things in life that we have limits with.
Oftentimes, we don't realize what our boundaries
actually are because they are just a part of life. We do
this. We don't do that. We set boundaries with our time,
in relationships, and to protect our families. Boundaries
are everywhere. Yet, we don't really find out how
important they are until we're in unexpected
circumstances like seasons of waiting. Since situations
like these come so unexpectedly it is important to know

what your personal boundaries and family boundaries are, so that when unexpected days arrive you can thrive and not fall into the temptations that life can so easily bring. Boundaries provide us protection and a safe place to simply be, while all the other things of life are outside our control.

I didn't know I had boundaries. The people-pleaser in me said yes to everything and everyone. When we began our season of waiting, we were brand new missionaries on the ground in Central America. Our three-month trip suddenly had no end date in sight. We were thrown into a completely new culture leaving me to relearn even the most basic skills of day-to-day life. The new language in itself was enough stress to leave me overwhelmed and just barely getting by. The boundaries I didn't know I had and didn't know I needed were crossed daily and I never even realized it. People would walk into our home and sit on the couch for hours upon hours. They would invite themselves over for meals creating more stress and anxiousness in my heart. Their excitement for the new family in the neighborhood was my breaking point. I never felt I could say no to the overwhelming needs of the people we were sent to serve so we would give everything we had only to be left completely empty. It all started with the people-pleaser in me but being unaware of my own boundaries caused me to spiral into grief and depression on top of the disappointment that led us to our waiting. I was exactly where God wanted us to be, but I was dying on the inside. The introvert in me was screaming for a moment of peace but my lack of boundaries was so tied to my identity that the only way I knew how to live during this season was to put everyone else first and quietly die on the inside. Those boundaries overflowed into every area of my life during that time. They spiraled and spiraled from one poor decision to another causing me to glue on a happy face over the pain that was going on inside my heart.

It reminds me of Sarah and Abraham in the Bible. The Lord spoke to Abraham telling him that He was going to be the father of many nations even though he had zero children at that time. The Lord invited them to enter the waiting zone. The promise was coming, but just like the rest of us, they got impatient. When God doesn't deliver in our time frame, we tend to try to take things into our own hands. It all goes back to that saying, "God helps those who help themselves." When God tells us to wait, we often come to the conclusion in our mind that God is the one waiting on us. So, what does Abraham and Sarai do? They take the situation into their own hands. Sarai decides that her maidservant will carry her children. And Abraham goes right along with the plan. They acted out of their impatience and frustration and then they got angry when their plan turned out the way they wanted it to. Any other time, Sarai probably would not have given her maid servant to her husband to conceive a child, but she had received a promise from the Lord, and she wanted it in her timing. Her choice overflowed into some dangerous territory all because she decided that she needed to take things into her own hands. She let go of her boundaries and fixed her eyes on what she could control. Searching for the desires of her heart left her to pick up the pieces of the choices she made.

You have boundaries whether you realize it or not. This is the time to rediscover those boundaries. Way too often when we're waiting on God for extended periods of time we start doubting and wonder if we heard Him correctly. We make decisions based on the things we *can* control or do about the situation. We pray that God would just get us out of it instead of surrendering and worshiping through the wait. We give in to things that we normally wouldn't. Today you have the opportunity to reevaluate your boundaries. Decide what is working and what is not for you and for your family. Boundaries are created so that we remain protected through every season. Sometimes those boundaries need to be tighter during days of waiting. You can wait well. Do not let the decisions you make today lead you to an Ishmael. Pursue righteousness through every moment along this journey. Do not give in to temptation whatever that may be for you. Do not doubt what God has spoken over your situation. Read Genesis Chapters 15-18 today. Walk away from the distractions and sit with Jesus. Let Him realign the places of your heart that are striving for control. Be encouraged that even though you may have made some bad decisions along the way that God will be faithful to do what He has promised. Wait on the Lord.

Day Four
The Blessing of Protection

So the king gave the order, and they brought Daniel and threw him into the lions' den. The king said to Daniel, "May your God, whom you serve continually, rescue you!
Daniel 6:16 HCSB

The waiting can feel dark and heavy. It can feel as if you are all alone with nowhere to go and no one to turn to. It can feel like unanswered prayers. It can feel hopeless. It can feel as if all clarity and answers have disappeared. It can feel as if God walked away and left you in complete silence. It's during these times when it is more important than ever to hold on to Jesus. You can know God and know the Bible and still end up in this place of utter despair. It's during these times of uncertainty when the things inside of us start to come out. The fear, depression, anger, and grief can all come swirling to the surface. Suddenly everything we know to be true flies out the window, leaving only our emotions of what we see to consume every minute of our days. Where is God? Why isn't He doing anything? Does He even hear me? Does He even care? Questions upon questions can leave us overwhelmed and problem focused.

But there is hope. During my days of waiting there was a long period of time where everything within me and everything outside of me looked and felt like I was dying. There was no hope. God wasn't speaking to me, so I thought. He wasn't moving any mountains. He wasn't changing my circumstances. He wasn't making rivers in the desert. Nothing was happening except this spiral into depression and grief. I knew all the scripture. I knew He would never leave me or forsake me. My head knew it but, for some reason it got lost in my heart. I remember crying out to God daily and sometimes every minute simply asking where He was. During this time, He began to slowly, but surely reintroduce Himself to me. He took this place of defeat and feelings of failure and He started working His way back into my life, through months and months of emotional roller coaster rides. He finally broke through and reminded me that He hadn't actually gone anywhere. He led me to Psalms 57 and something broke off in my thinking. All this time, I had been thinking that this dark, lonely place of isolation was a pit. Yet, He was actually hiding me in the shadow of His wings. There were things inside of me that needed to be dealt with, healed, restored, and renewed.

Some of these things are only able to be dealt with during times of waiting. It's in these seasons of waiting that God has us exactly where He wants us. This place is exactly where He needs us. It's during this time that He brings us to a place of total surrender that allows Him to uproot the things in our lives that need to be taken care of. The things that are keeping us from moving forward and keeping us from being all He has created us to be. These times are dark, not because we're all alone, but because He has us tucked up inside of Him. The waiting gives us a safe place to let Him work within us. The shadow of His wing gives us the freedom to simply be. We fight it because it's uncomfortable to be stripped of everything we hold dear. Yet, if we truly knew everything that He was doing during this time of darkness we would be amazed at how good He is. The shadow of His wing protects us from the outside world. Sometimes we're in the situations we're in because God is so much greater than we know. These days that feel hopeless are not there to harm you but are actually there to strengthen you and increase your faith for the days ahead.

My waiting came because I said yes to Jesus. I surrendered myself to His will and followed Him across the nations to rescue a little girl and call her my own. My waiting came, because the paperwork we needed to allow us to return home didn't come when I thought it should. It left us thousands of miles away, raising a baby in a third world country with no family and friends nearby. It didn't come by choice, yet here we are stuck needing the greatest miracle of our lives. It reminds me of Daniel in the lion's den in Daniel 6. Daniel found himself in the lion's den, not because he did something wrong, but because he did something right. He remained faithful to God even when he knew there were consequences. His choice was either to give in to the demands of his enemies or to remain faithful even unto death. He chose to remain faithful and found himself in a dark pit surrounded by hungry lions.

Daniel 6:22 tells us that God sent angels to shut the lion's mouths. God protected Daniel, because he was found innocent before Him. Daniel's time in the lion's den was short. But I'm guessing that that pit did not feel like a place of safety for Daniel. He was left waiting on God to deliver him. Little did Daniel know that the lion's den was the safest place for him to be at the time. That dark pit was God's protection for Daniel. It was the blessing of protection that led Daniel to prosperity. It was Daniel's testimony that led King Darius to glorify and honor the One True Living God. I don't know how your waiting came to be or how long you have been waiting. I do know that if you have been feeling like you're in a dark place, you can be encouraged. Take another look at your circumstances. God is moving even when you don't feel like He is. More than likely, He has you wrapped up in the shadow of His wing, protecting you from things you see and even the things you don't see. Do not lose hope. Take time today to read through Psalms 57 and Daniel 6. Remind yourself that your Heavenly Father is delivering you. There are great blessings found in His protection.

Day Five
When Everything is Shaken

This expression, 'Yet once more,' indicates the removal of what can be shaken - that is, created things - so that what is not shaken might remain. Therefore, since we are receiving a kingdom that cannot be shaken, let us hold on to grace. By it, we may serve God acceptably, with reverence and awe, for our God is a consuming fire.
Hebrews 12:27-29 HCSB

There is something about new unknown seasons that leave every part of us uncomfortable. Especially when entering a new and unknown season was not by your own choice. New seasons are usually a good thing. By the end of Spring, we're usually overjoyed to enter into summer. By the end of summer, we're usually excited to experience the cool fall days. Then from those cool fall days it's time to jump into winter to sit in front of a cozy fire surrounded by those we love. Then, once more, it is back to Spring to watch the flowers bloom and life begin to grow again. Yet, seasons in the wilderness are a different story. Uninhabited land often has a mind of its own. Things grow differently there. The signs of changing seasons we're familiar with don't meet our expectations in the wilderness. Seasons in the wilderness seem to last longer. The seeds planted take longer to bear fruit. The trees may be barren longer than expected. It's in the silence of those confusing unknown seasons where who we think we are gets tested.

During our time in the wilderness, we were living in the middle of the jungle in Central America. It was honestly one place I never pictured our family living. The jungle is a different type of wilderness. It constantly taught me lessons. One year the rainy season was more than late. Our well was completely dry. The city's water supply was empty. We were in a completely different culture doing what God had called us to do and raising a one-year-old when we found ourselves without water. There were no longer any showers, no dishes, and no laundry. It was the picture of everything going on internally. Now, a year into our waiting and it was also going on externally. We needed yet another miracle just to live a normal life with water. The rain was so late that year that we went an entire month without water. At this point into our journey, I honestly didn't think I could break anymore. And yet once again, I found myself on my knees unable to stand. Fear was holding me hostage. The fears of just trying to survive. The fears of caring for a child through it all. The fears of the enemies we were facing as we fought for our miracle. The list of fears went on and on. The fear was crippling. It felt like this one season of many seasons in the wilderness was never ending. It was during this time where everything within me felt like it was being shaken.

I would stay up late after everyone else had gone to sleep, turn on the worship music, fall on my knees, and just lay there and cry. I would just wait there on my knees until the Lord would come. The Holy Spirit would always show up even if it wasn't how I wanted or expected. It was during that time where He began to work on my heart. It was after I stopped denying that this was a season of waiting. It was after I sat back and acknowledged that He was still with me. It was after I completely surrendered to this very uncomfortable process of waiting. It was after all these things that He met me there on my knees. It was there that He began to bring all these things to the surface that I needed to deal with. Things that had nothing to do with the situation I was in. Things that had nothing to do with the waiting. Things that I had stuffed down deep inside my heart that I had refused to deal with. Things that I hadn't surrendered to the Lord. It was in those meetings with the Holy Spirit night after night, crying on my knees, where I could feel Him shaking me and peeling things off of me.

Doubt, fear, worry, anxiety, depression, grief, and pride were just a few of the things that I needed to be real and honest with God about. For so long, all the emotions of the wait had piled up deep inside of me and left me painting on a smile for myself, for everyone around me, and to God. Of course, He knows us better than we know ourselves. He knit us together in our mother's womb. How silly it is to think we can hide things from Him. But it was in those nights of surrender, in those nights of shaking, where the Holy Spirit took everything that wasn't of Him and stripped me of all I thought I knew myself to be. It was through the process of surrendering all the things from years and years of wrong thinking and the false identity I had given myself where He returned me to Himself. It was one of the most painful processes of losing myself. But it was in losing myself that God began to rebuild my foundation in Him. A foundation that could never be shaken.

His voice shook the earth at that time, but now He has promised, Yet once more I will shake not only the earth but also heaven. This expression, 'Yet once more,' indicates the removal of what can be shaken - that is created things - so that what is not shaken might remain. Therefore, since we are receiving a kingdom that cannot be shaken, let us hold on to grace. By it, we may serve God acceptably, with reverence and awe, for our God is a consuming fire.
Hebrews 12:26-29 HCSB

God wants to do so much more than that miracle you are waiting for. He's more concerned with your heart than just giving you the one thing you think will make everything better. This time is more about the process than it is the gift. God wants to use this time to shake away everything that is not from Him so that your foundation can be sure, steady, and unshakable. One of the greatest lessons I've learned in the waiting is that our greatest 'yes' to God is not actually a yes at all if we're saying yes to other things. Will you say yes to meeting with Him today? Will you let Him shake off the broken places of your life so that He can rebuild a foundation that cannot be shaken? It's in the shaking where the process of healing and restoration begins. Spend some time reading Hebrews 12 today. Ask the Holy Spirit to show you the areas of your life that you need to surrender to Him. I pray that your foundation would be unshakable and that your heart would be encouraged and strengthened as the Lord heals the deepest places of your heart.

Day Six
Deep Roots

Enlarge the site of your tent, and let your tent
curtains be stretched out; do not hold back;
lengthen your ropes, and drive your pegs deep.
Isaiah 54:2 HCSB

My waiting took place in the literal jungle. It's
one of the most beautiful places you can imagine, but it
also comes with the greatest headaches. When our
daughter was born, we were living in a small village in
Central America. Knowing that we would need a miracle
to return home as a family we continued to say yes to
following Jesus through the miracle process. We were
already planning to live short term in this jungle before
we knew the size of the miracle we were waiting on.
Yet, my greatest fear was finding out that our daughter
was in fact going to be born in that jungle. A jungle,
hours from an airport, away from our family, where
everyone spoke a different language. It wasn't quite the
picture of happily ever after I had imagined when I
pictured bringing that little bundle of joy home. But
there we were following after Jesus and what He had
spoken over our lives. I have often thought our wait
started in that jungle, but as I think back, our wait

actually started years before when the Holy Spirit first spoke to us about the promise He had placed on our lives. The intensity of our wait started in the jungle though, as door after door closed in the paperwork, we needed to head home as a family. We had so much faith that God was going to do what He said, but we wrapped up that gift with our own thoughts, timelines and expectations. Day after day as we watched things get more and more impossible our faith decreased and fear increased. We were all alone in the wilderness with no hope.

It took me a long time to realize what God was doing to our roots during this time. Honestly, it took years for me to realize what was happening. While there have been days, I have absolutely hated that jungle I can tell you now that it is one of the things, I am most thankful for in life. One of the things I love about the jungle are the trees. It only takes a short drive out of town to be in the middle of the jungle surrounded by the biggest trees you've ever seen. Some of the tree trunks are bigger than cars. Yet, some of the tallest trees have the tiniest trunks. Regardless of their size everything stays green in the jungle. All year round, as fruit comes and goes, it's still green. Something is always growing even through the longest droughts. As I would work in the garden and out in the yard, one thing caught my attention over and over again. Even though everything is green, the soil is as hard as a rock. You have to dig and dig through hard, clay, rocky ground to get to the roots. With the ground being so hard and dry it makes it almost impossible to transplant anything. The ground is so dry that most of the rain is immediately sucked up by the dirt, leaving the ground looking as if it was never even wet. So how can the jungle remain so green in an environment that looks so impossible for growth? It all comes back to the roots. One thing I noticed during the waiting was how shallow my roots were. I grew up in church. I knew Jesus since I was a little girl, but I didn't know Him the way a daughter knows her father. My identity had been so wrapped up in the world that after the Lord stripped me of everything, I knew myself to be, it left my roots barely hanging on. My foundation needed serious work and it was only through the waiting process that God had gotten my full attention. It was only through the reconstruction of my foundation that I was going to be able to grow and thrive after the waiting.

When our roots, our foundation, is established deep in Jesus, it doesn't matter what the circumstances or situations around us are. We will continue to grow and thrive. Wilderness seasons often leave us feeling as if we've been left alone in the dark, but more often than not, it is in those seasons where we have been planted. Your wilderness may not be a literal jungle, but if you are waiting you are in the wilderness none the less. It's in this place where God wants to enlarge your territory like it talks about in Isaiah 54. God wants to strengthen your stakes and lengthen your cords so that your roots are placed so firmly in Him that nothing or no one will be able to hurt your foundation. It's the wilderness where Jesus helps our roots grow so deep in knowing Him that it allows us to continue to grow strong through all the other seasons of life. He is the rock and our firm foundation. Will you let Him deepen your roots today? He wants you to thrive in every season. He wants your identity to be based on who He says you are as His son or daughter. There is purpose in your wait today. Spend today reading through Isaiah 54. If the stripping and shaking of your life has left you drained, today you can be encouraged that your roots are growing deeper. You will prosper in every way as your soul prospers. You will withstand every battle with an unmovable, unshakable, strong foundation in the author and finisher of your faith.

> *The rain fell, the rivers rose, and the winds blew*
> *and pounded that house. Yet it didn't collapse,*
> *because its foundation was on the rock.*
> *Matthew 7:25 HCSB*

Day Seven
Discovering What Remains

Coastlands, listen to me; distant peoples, pay attention. The LORD called me before I was born. He named me while I was in my mother's womb.
Isaiah 49:1 HCSB

I had "Isaiah 49:16" tattooed on my wrist long before I ever grasped the magnitude of the connection between my life and Isaiah 49. This piece of scripture has been a constant reminder to me, over the last decade, of who I am in Christ. I am a servant of the Lord and the daughter of a King. I actually got the tattoo before God shook me to my core. It was my constant reminder that even if everyone else forgot about me that He never would. And then I entered the waiting. That was when everything I knew started to shake and my false identity made itself known. It was in the beginning of my waiting where God went silent. At times it even seemed like He had walked away. Day after day, looking down at my wrist, fighting anger and grief, I began to read Isaiah 49 once more. I would read it day after day just waiting for God to meet me in that place. Soon, I realized what He was doing. Verse 2 and 3 says,

"*He made my words like a sharp sword; He hid me in the shadow of His hand. He made me like a sharpened arrow; He hid me in His quiver. He said to me, 'You are My Servant, Israel; I will be glorified in him.'*" HCSB

It was through this scripture that something clicked, and I was reminded that He hadn't left, but had me tucked up safe and secure in His hand.

The process is never easy. It usually leads to a place of isolation, making a dark situation even heavier. Whether you were diagnosed with an illness, lost a job, or are waiting for a loved one to come back to Jesus, the process can be downright brutal. Yet, it is in this process, after everything has been stripped from you that those deep roots can begin to take hold. It is only then that the process of discovering what remains begins. When you remove the worldly thoughts of who you are; unloved, unwanted and unseen, then you can discover the person that God says you are. Our old identity will gradually be shattered over time. Words people have spoken over us, our acceptance of worldly cultures, our bad choices and wrong mindsets slowly shift how we see ourselves over time. We tend to build our identities on things of this world instead of renewing our minds to see ourselves the way God created us. It is in the silence of the wilderness that we are able to recognize what God is actually delivering us from. Anger, grief, doubt, insecurities, self-hatred, shame, or whatever label you have given yourself is not who you are. Once these things have been stripped from you and the branches have been cut off it can often times leave your heart feeling empty. It is in that place of surrender, when you have nothing, that God can begin to heal you, fill you and build a foundation that cannot be shaken. A foundation that restores your view of who God is, the God of the Bible. Not the God of that YouTube video you just watched, not the God of theology, or who your neighbor says God is, but the God of Abraham, Isaac, and Jacob. The God of covenant. The Creator of the Universe. It is when everything is taken away that you will embark on the adventure of discovering what truly remains. Isaiah 49 says that God gave you your name while you were in your mother's womb. Before you were born, He called you as His son or daughter. Who you are and who He created you to be can only be found in Him.

God created you. He formed you in your mother's womb. He knew your first breath and He knows your last. Nothing can be hidden from Him. He is your Father, your provider, your counselor and your friend. He adopted you as His own. You are chosen. You are loved. You are seen. His heart is for you to know Him and to know who you are in Him. He will not leave you empty. You have a choice today to embark on an adventure with Him. I encourage you to write down everything you think about who you are, then go through your Bible and write down beside it everything God says you are. Recognize the lies. Surrender those things to Him and ask Him to renew your mind and your heart so that you can see yourself the way He sees you. This process of waiting is more about your heart than what you are waiting for. This time is about what God is doing inside of you. He is more than capable to give you what you're waiting for. Nothing is impossible for Him. Yet, it is the time in the wilderness when He heals us, restores us, matures, us, and prepares us for what is next. Do not think that this time is wasted. Do not think that it has no purpose. The foundation that is being built is more valuable than what your heart is longing for right now. If you have a life verse or a passage of scripture that you run to spend time soaking in those words today. Remind yourself of who God is and who God says you are. If you do not have a life verse read Isaiah 49 today. Spend time sitting in silence and let God begin to fill you heart and mind with your true identity. You are a son or a daughter before you are anything else. It's time to let go and embrace who you were truly created to be.

The below is also a great statement to read out loud, declaring who you really are.

- I am a child of the King, an heir of God and a joint heir with Christ.
- I am more than a conqueror through Him that loves me.
- Fear has no permanent place in my life, because God has not given me a spirit of fear.
- I am confident that no spiritual weapon that is used against me will prosper because God is for me, so who can be against me?

- Every curse spoken against me is powerless because I am blessed.
- I am blessed coming in and blessed going out.
- I am blessed with good gifts that I have not earned and cannot lose.
- I am blessed because God knew my name before I was born.
- I am blessed because I am being transformed into the image of Christ.
- I have been made Holy and Blameless in the eyes of God by the Blood of Christ.
- My enemies shall come against me one way and God will cause them to flee in seven ways.
- I am blessed because God Himself delights in me and rejoices over me with singing.
- All the people in my life shall see that I am called by the name of the Lord.
- I am persuaded that neither death, nor life, nor angels, nor principalities, nor powers, nor things present, nor things to come, nor height, nor depth, nor any other creature shall be able to separate me from the love of my God.

Day Eight
Pursuing Righteousness

*For I have kept the ways of the LORD and have not
turned from my God to wickedness. Indeed, I have kept
all His ordinances in mind and have not disregarded
His statues. I was blameless before Him and kept myself
from sinning. So the LORD repaid me according to my
righteousness, according to my cleanness in His sight.
2 Samuel 22:22-25 HCSB*

Today is a good day to have a good day. There is
so much that God wants to do in your heart during this
time to heal you, restore you and increase you. He
wants you to know Him. Maybe you're waiting for God
to show you the next step or maybe you're still on your
knees praying for breakthrough. It really doesn't matter
what day of waiting you're on because every day of
waiting needs you to intentionally pursue
righteousness. For several years I was constantly on a
plane and in and out of airports. So, what happens when
you travel? You wait a lot. Flights rarely leave and arrive
on time. There are lines for the bathroom, restaurants,
coffee and boarding. Weather impacts your waiting,
crowds impact your waiting and even the things you

bring along with you impact your waiting. Some people accomplish so much while they are traveling, they continue working and creating. As for me I have never been one of those people. I always haul all my work stuff thinking that this may be the trip where I'll accomplish something and every time something happens, and I never pull out the computer. When traveling develops in a way you never planned, which it often does, it's too easy to sit and scroll social media or watch another movie. It's easier to zone out than it is to be intentional on what you've planned to do. It's the same in the wilderness.

Grief, uncertainty, depression, bitterness, or even just a lack of clarity can lead into a downward spiral. It is easy to spend your days waiting on the couch. It's easier to watch another movie, binge watch Netflix, or keep up with everyone else's life on Facebook. All of those feelings can leave you frozen. You're unsure of the days ahead and maybe even a little terrified to see what the day will bring. Maybe you're physically unable to get off the couch. Maybe you haven't been able to stop crying. Maybe your emotions are fine but you're not sure what you're supposed to be doing in this awkward season of your life. I spent so many days battling the emotions of the trauma in my life that, for over a year, I couldn't accomplish a single thing. I was looking back through pictures of the birth of my daughter and it's funny because from the pictures everything looked amazing. There were smiles and a new bundle of joy. Yet, the memories were filled with crippling fear. We were in a third world country and unable to speak the language very well. I had parasites for the first two weeks of my daughter's life leaving me unable to eat or drink anything. We lived in three hotels during the first six weeks of her life. Then we experienced the greatest disappointment of our lives when we found out that the paperwork, we needed to take her home was not going to happen when we thought it would. We knew we were going to need a miracle. When God didn't do the impossible in the way we thought and when we thought He would, we completely fell apart. The birth day pictures wouldn't show you that though. The trauma and grief we experienced left us crippled. If I could just order food to be delivered to our hotel room, I felt like that was an accomplishment for me during that time. Pursuing righteousness was the last thing on my mind.

I don't know where you are today. I don't know what you're waiting looks like. I don't know if you're experiencing total despair or if you're excited about your journey through the wilderness. What I do know is today you have a choice. Will you zone out once more and search for anything normal or comfortable, or will you embrace where God has you and search for Him in this journey? You can sit and watch another movie, or you can turn on a sermon. You can blast worldly music, or you can fall on your face and worship. You can scan Facebook for the latest gossip, or you can reach out to a friend who is going to encourage you and lift you up. Pursuing righteousness is not the easy choice, but it is the one that will heal you, restore you and bring you closer to Jesus. The choices you make today will greatly impact the rest of your waiting season. Pursuing righteousness is not just a choice for today, but a choice that you will need to make every day. Will you choose to surrender daily? Will you choose to be honest and vulnerable with the Lord? It's okay to tell Him that you have no idea what He's doing, that you don't understand, that you are struggling to trust Him, that you are hurting. He knows you and He sees you. Invite Him in to do whatever He wants to do in your heart today. Search for scriptures on righteousness. Write them down and post them around your house. What does it mean? What does it look like for you today? Choose to do hard things and run after righteousness.

But you, man of God, run from these things, and pursue righteousness, godliness, faith, love, endurance, and gentleness. Fight the good fight for the faith; take hold of eternal life that you were called to and have made a good confession about in the presence of many witnesses.
1 Timothy 6:11-12 HCSB

Day Nine
The Cost of Discipleship

*Whoever finds his life will lose it, and
whoever loses his life for my sake will find it.*
Matthew 10:39 ESV

Today is a critical day in your waiting. It doesn't
matter if you found yourself waiting because of
situations outside your control or if you sold all your
stuff and embarked on this season of waiting in
obedience to the call God has placed on your life. It
doesn't matter if today, you find yourself trying
desperately to hold the pieces of your life together or if
this season of waiting has been a nice change of pace. It
doesn't matter what day of waiting you are on. It
doesn't matter if you don't see breakthrough in sight.
Today is critical. Today you need to know or be
reminded that there is a cost to following Jesus. You
need to know that when you give your life to Jesus you
are saying no to everything else so that you can say yes
to Him. Luke 14:25-33 goes as far to say that you have
to be willing to lay aside your mother, father, sister,
brother, spouse and even your own life to be a disciple
of Jesus. This can be an incredibly hard reality in the
wilderness. It's easy to agree to give your life away

when you still hold everything in your hands. But when you are in the wilderness and everything has been stripped away things get serious.

It brings you back to that day you said yes, that day you first gave your heart to Jesus. You may still be dealing with anger, confusion or bitterness from the shaking in your life. You may be left wondering what comes next or wondering if you correctly heard the call to surrender it all to Him. Regardless, today is a critical day for you to, once again, decide if you are going to continue to say yes to Jesus. Today is the day you need to decide if you are going to surrender everything, once more. Will you lay down your emotions, the heaviness and the doubt? Will you return to your first love? Will you say yes to do whatever it takes and give whatever it costs to glorify God with your life?

The biggest trial my husband and I faced in our season of waiting was leaving behind our families to follow Jesus. It was much easier when we thought it was for a short three months. But as weeks and months went on and breakthrough seemed more and more impossible by the day, we soon realized that God had thrown our timeline out the window. He wasn't coming when we wanted Him to or when we thought He would. We were trapped with no way home to our families. That was when we started to truly realize what the cost of discipleship was. We could believe in Jesus all day long, but it came to a point where we had to decide if we were willing to give whatever it costs to be His disciples. We left behind mothers, fathers, grandparents, brothers, and sons. It has been the hardest thing for us in following God into the waiting. To lay them aside so that we could say yes to God shattered our hearts in so many ways. It was so difficult knowing we would miss birthdays, holidays, sick days and every day in between. To trust Jesus with their lives while we were a million miles away was a new level of trust we had to walk through. Our love for them grew through every passing day, yet we had a critical point in the waiting to decide if the cost was worth it. If leaving everything behind to follow after Jesus was worth the cost or if we were going to pack our bags and search for life on our own. You may not be facing a situation where you have to leave your family behind, yet at some point in this journey through the wilderness you are going to be faced with the choice of deciding if the cost is worth it.

Whoever loves father or mother more than me is not worthy of me, and whoever loves son or daughter more than me is not worthy of me. And whoever does not take his cross and follow me is not worthy of me. Whoever finds his life will lose it, and whoever loses his life for my sake will find it.
Matthew 10:37-39 ESV

What do you need to lay aside today so that you can say yes to Jesus once more? What do you need to surrender? It might not be your family. It might be worry or fear. It might be a promotion at work. Maybe it is believing your doctor over what Jesus says. Our deepest and greatest joy comes from knowing God and being deeply known by Him. Will you lose your life today so that you can find it? Will you follow Him into the deep unknown so that He can do one of the greatest miracles in your life? The miracles you're asking for always begin with you, giving your life away. The greatest advice I can give you during your waiting is to lay down your life. Lay aside everything you hold dear and cling tightly to Jesus. Everything you need is in Him. He is your portion. He alone is your hope. There is purpose in your waiting. He sees the big picture. He will restore everything that was lost. Will you let Him show it to you? Spend some time alone today worshiping Jesus. Make a list of everything that the Holy Spirit shows you that you need to lay aside. Surrender those things today and make an intentional decision to say, "Yes, whatever it takes and whatever it costs, I will lay down my life for the glory of Jesus." He is worthy.

Day Ten
A Life Laid Down

*And they have conquered him by the blood
of the Lamb and by the word of their testimony,
for they loved not their lives even unto death.
Revelation 12:11 ESV*

This verse in Revelation 12 is quoted a lot. I've heard songs about it and have seen it on shirts. It's the hope of a lot of sermons. Yet, the second half of it is normally cut off. We overcome by the blood of the Lamb and the word of our testimony! What a promise! The last part doesn't really matter though, right? You know the, "for they loved not their lives even unto death" part. We live in such an amazing society that truly takes so much for granted. We have everything we want at the tips of our fingers. It's the microwave effect of having instantaneous blessings overflowing in every aspect of our lives. It's so great to have money in the bank, a house that we can decorate to feel like home and so much food in the fridge that we can't decide what to eat so we order out. It's the American dream. You don't have to make a fortune to still reap the rewards of those things. We've become so comfortable in living well that we've lost sight of the true call of the gospel to come and die. The true call to *love not our lives even unto death.* The call of the gospel to lay down our lives so that God's will can be done in and through us.

What does it look like to lay your life down? Most of us currently do not face the persecution that some of our brothers and sisters around the world do. We're not currently being thrown in jail or being beheaded because of our faith. And while one day we may be faced with the choice to save our life or die in the name of Jesus, that is not happening today. So what could it possibly look like to lay down our lives for Jesus today? What does it mean to *love not our lives even unto death*? How does it fit into our season of waiting on God? It reminds me of the widow's offering parable in Mark.

And he sat down opposite the treasury and watched the people putting money into the offering box. Many rich people put in large sums. And a poor widow came and put in two small copper coins, which make a penny. And he called his disciples to him and said to them, "Truly, I say to you, this poor widow has put in more than all those who are contributing to the offering box. For they all contributed out of their abundance, but she out of her poverty has put in everything she had, all she had to live on. Mark 12:41-44 ESV

This is a life laid down. This is what *loving not your life unto death* could look like.

When we moved to the mission field and then got extremely delayed on our return date as we waited for our daughter's paperwork to be able to travel back, we experienced a lot of ups and downs in our funding. After being gone over a year, losing touch with people and flat out being too exhausted to think, we lost a lot of financial support. It caused us to walk through a couple months of crippling fear as we were stuck in a third world country with shaky internet access, no family to lean on, and a savings account that was draining drastically. My identity as a daughter of God relied heavily on the mindset that if I have everything I want that God is providing for me. If I have all the money to pay my bills, food in the fridge, and a savings account then God still loves me the way I think He does. But then everything stopped. People walked away, funds stopped coming in, and everything I thought that proved God was our provider came crashing down. It was months of asking God, "Where did you go?" I questioned and blamed myself for not stewarding well. I thought that I should be doing more to generate revenue. Yet, it wasn't about that at all. The fear brought me to a point where I had to lay my life down. I knew God called us there to bring this baby into our home. We were being obedient, but I couldn't understand why everything around us was crashing down.

It took several months for God to get my attention and remind me that I said yes to Him. It was during this time, in the waiting, that I had to decide if I was going to continue to say yes and lay my life down for Jesus. I knew He was doing something inside of me far larger than my mind could grasp at that point, but it was so painful watching him tear apart my foundation. He was growing me up in Christ and it was up to me if I was going to, once again, give Him everything. I looked at what I had in my hands and said, "Lord, here's my life. Here's every part of it. Make something beautiful that glorifies you."

Sometimes *loving not your life even unto death* looks like letting go of the things that make you, you. Or letting go of the things that cause fear, worry and depression to make an appearance in your life. Sometimes, it's letting go of the mindset of why and how you live like you live. Sometimes it's letting go of the constant need to control and understand why something is happening in your life. Whatever it is, today is the day where you choose, once again, to lay your life down. Will you let go and surrender the parts you don't understand? Will you admit that this process of waiting is not about you but about what God is doing inside of you for His glory? God was still providing for us, even though it wasn't what I was used to or how I wanted it to be. He was always faithful. Today I operate differently because my foundation has been rebuilt on Jesus, the solid rock on which I can stand. Read through the story of the widow's offering today. Are you willing to give it all away? Will you love Jesus more than you love your own life? He's so worthy of your all. Worthy is the Lamb who was slain. May you *love not your life even unto death*.

I wait for the Lord,
my soul waits,
and in his word I hope;
Psalms 130:5 ESV

Day Eleven
Whispers In The Night

And the LORD called again, "Samuel!" and Samuel arose
and went to Eli and said, "Here I am, for you called me."
But he said, "I did not call, my son; lie down again."
Now Samuel did not yet know the LORD, and the word
of the LORD had not yet been revealed to him.
1 Samuel 3:6-7 ESV

Before I entered the wait, I was blessed with time
to sit at the feet of Jesus every day. I did most of my
work from home while my husband served the
homeless and the Church out on the streets every day.
We didn't have any kids then, which left my days quiet.
It would bring me so much joy to go into our spare
bedroom where my piano was and sit and worship and
write for hours. Now looking back, I took so much of
that time for granted. It was so easy to enter into His
presence in that room. The warfare was intense at times
but the peace those hours brought were something I
will never forget. When the Lord told us to pack up and
leave our home to start a new adventure overseas with
Him, the hardest part was leaving that space where He

met me every day. Giving away my stuff was the easy part. Giving away my guitar and piano was sad, but the hardest part was walking away from that room. That place that I knew He would always be. The place I knew He would always meet me. Yet, I knew God was calling me to let go and follow Him and that is exactly what I did.

It sounds weird to say, but it took a long time for me to find that space with Him once more. I honestly never thought it would be so hard to find Him again. We left our home and moved overseas, and our wait began immediately. We were thrown into a different adventure than we had originally planned, and the lack of clarity mixed with a new culture and language left my heart in disarray. I was exhausted by the tiniest things, because my heart was so desperate for Jesus. I went months of being busy and exhausted and couldn't hear His voice. I was trying desperately to survive all the new things and the bad news after bad news that was thrown our way. I knew He had called us to this place. I knew He was there with us even though at times I doubted. I had all the prophetic words written down, yet I couldn't find that place I had with Him back home.

It reminded me of Samuel in 1 Samuel 3. The LORD called Samuel in the middle of the night multiple times, yet Samuel did not recognize His voice. He questioned Eli every time and Eli would tell him to go back to bed. Finally, Eli realized what was going on and told Samuel that it was the LORD who was calling him. This was the first time that Samuel had experienced the

LORD. It was completely out of the ordinary and I'm sure it looked nothing like Samuel thought His first experience with the LORD was going to look like. If the wait has taught me anything, it has taught me that God can speak to us, engage us, minister to us and show His power to us in any way He wants to. When we walk into the wilderness, we tend to depend on encountering God the way we always have. When everything else seems out of control, we try to cling to the things we can control. It leaves us putting God in a box and many times can cause us to miss hearing His voice because we are looking for Him in a specific way at a specific time. It took months of me complaining to God that I couldn't hear Him before I finally turned on the worship music and fell to my knees in the middle of the night. I surrendered my will and told God to come however He wanted to. The moment I let Him come out of the box that my mind had placed Him in was when He began reintroducing Himself to me. He didn't come in the way I wanted Him to or when I wanted Him to. He didn't speak to me in long profound words that made all the confusion go away, but He came. He shook off all the things I thought I knew about Him and began rebuilding my foundation. A foundation that could never be shaken.

It's common in the wait to experience a lot of silence. Sometimes that silence is much too loud. It causes all our thoughts, emotions and fear to start swirling to the surface. All those things can cause us to miss what the Holy Spirit is doing. But it is in the wait and the silence where the world is removed that God in His loving kindness can reintroduce Himself to us. If you have been looking for Him in a specific way, I highly encourage you to let go of your expectations and let Him meet you however He wants to. Your time with Him most likely looks different now than it did then. You've had to let go, readjust and redefine your life. The same is true now in how you make time to read your Bible, worship and sit at the feet of Jesus. It won't look the same. It doesn't have to look the same. You will find purpose in the new. Listen for the whispers of the Holy Spirit. The whispers may come in the middle of the night, while you're washing dishes or while you're out for a walk. The key is to allow the silence to be the gateway for this new adventure with Him. He has not abandoned you, but He is waiting for you to accept that things are different now. It will be good for you, and it will bring Him glory! Will you trust Him today? Will you lay down the old and embrace the new? I promise He will meet you there. Read the story of God talking to Samuel in 1 Samuel 3 today. You may not recognize His voice at first but keep pressing in as you experience the fullness of His presence.

Day Twelve
A Living Sacrifice

*Therefore, brother, by the mercies of God, I urge you
to present your bodies as a living sacrifice, holy and
pleasing to God; this is your spiritual worship. Do not
be conformed to this age, but be transformed by the
renewing of your mind, so that you may discern
what is the good, pleasing, and perfect will of God.*
Romans 12:1-2 HCSB

Sacrifice is not a common word in our
vocabulary. It's something I think about when I listen to
testimonies or read books about Christians that have
died for their faith. But what is sacrifice to the average
person? What does the Bible mean when it talks about
presenting our bodies as a living sacrifice? The word
sacrifice not only feels uncomfortable, but slightly
terrifying as we ponder what we are going to lose in the
process. Could laying down our lives and sacrificing
what we hold dear possibly bring God glory? Could a
world that says, "Come and prosper." Have anything to
do with living as a sacrifice?

When I said yes to following Jesus into the
unknown, I knew I would be uncomfortable. I knew I

would be stretched. I knew I would have to let things go. What I didn't foresee was the sacrifice. What I prepared for was temporary, but as the wait dragged on so did the sacrifice. It was never on my bucket list to raise my daughter thousands of miles away from my family and friends, in a culture I didn't know, and a language I couldn't understand. The sacrifices that may seem minimal to some people, at the time left me feeling like I was losing everything. Sacrificing seems so much more painful when things are silent. The loss feels so much louder as hope feels deferred and disappointment sets in. It's easy to find sermons and scripture to fit the hopeful narrative that blessings look and feel like having everything you could ever dream of. It's so easy to enter into the trap of the enemy that says, "If God isn't giving me everything, I want then He's not good." Yet, we come back to the God of the Bible and discover that the gospel is, in fact, a message of, "Come follow me and die to yourself." In the dying and the sacrifice come the blessing.

This is not a message that most of us like to hear. Could we live in a manner that communicated to the world, "I love Jesus more than I love my own life." Could we follow Him into painful situations so that He can show the world just how good and powerful He is? Could we take a disease diagnosis, a job loss or simply the pains of everyday life and find joy in the trials? We pray for miracles every day, forgetting that we need an impossible situation for God to do the impossible. I remember the days where I begged God to see the impossible. I wanted so desperately to see dead things come to life, the lame to walk, the blind to see and the food to multiply. I wanted to see His power manifested every day of my life, but then the trials would come. They would bring pain, confusion, and depression and my heart would get stuck between the joy of seeing God's power and the overwhelming cares of the world.

I remember an outreach we did at the very beginning of our ministry. We had a small group of volunteers that were going out with us to a local park in Jacksonville, Florida to have a "Picnic in the Park" for the homeless. It was a Thanksgiving lunch where we would serve our street friends, share the gospel and love on those that would show up. We had no idea how many people would show up which makes planning an outreach like this quite stressful. It was our first time out so I think we planned for about twenty-five people to come and eat but brought food for fifty so that they could take food with them. Well, the word got out and we had over eighty people show up to eat. We did not have anywhere near enough food to feed everyone, and I was overwhelmed with stress and worry. The people-pleaser in me at the time was having a meltdown, thinking these people were going to be so angry with us. Just the thought that we were going to be sending people away hungry was devastating to me. The line was so long, but we prayed and got to work. I remember one of our volunteers telling me she just kept cutting the turkey and every time she cut some off more would need to be cut. The food multiplied right before our eyes. Not only did eighty people eat and eat well, but there were leftovers.

All I saw in the moment was the problem. We didn't have enough food and people were going to leave hungry. Honestly, in that moment, food multiplication wasn't even something I had asked for. I had people on standby ready to run down the street to the pizza place to get more food. I was so engulfed in the problem that was right in front of me that I couldn't see that God was about to do an incredible miracle. We could have sent someone for more food the moment we saw all the people show up, but something that day prompted us to wait and see.

Living as a sacrifice doesn't mean that you're going to spend the rest of your life in pain and problems. In fact, Proverbs 21:3 tells us,

Doing what is righteous and just is more acceptable to the LORD than sacrifice. HCSB

God is more concerned about your heart than He is about what you're laying down and giving up. Living as a sacrifice is simply getting out of the way. It's saying, "God this is what I'm seeing and feeling. I'm going to surrender these emotions, trust you with my life, and believe that you are going to do the impossible."

Will you ask God to renew your mind today? Can you take your eyes off the problems and fix them on Jesus? Present your body, your life, as a living sacrifice today. Pursue holiness and righteousness so that your faith increases as you wait on the Lord. Your heavenly Father sees the big picture. He knows what you've been through, what you're walking through, and what your future holds. Will you lay your problems at His feet so He can do the impossible? Jesus paid the ultimate sacrifice so that we can spend eternity with the Father. It is finished. He is so worthy of your all. Today, spend time praying specifically for God to renew your mind. Praise Him for all the impossible situations you see in front of you and then wait on Him as He does what only He can do.

Day Thirteen
Patiently Waiting

Rejoice in hope; be patient in
affliction; be persistent in prayer.
Romans 12:12: HCSB

Does anyone truly know how to be patient? The definition of patience according to google is: "The capacity to accept or tolerate delay, trouble, or suffering without getting angry or upset." Patience is not getting angry when we're not getting our way. Patience is waiting for God's perfect timing. Patience is being still and walking in peace when everything around us is spinning out of control. Patience is standing in righteousness when the rest of the world says that there's an easier way around this. I once heard a sermon that brought up the powerful point that if you don't have patience then you don't have love, because 1 Corinthians 13 says that love is patient. Ouch. Patience is a part of love. Patience is a lot of things. Yet, what patience meant to you before you entered the waiting compared to what it means to you now during the waiting is probably a completely different definition.

Before the wait, my definition of patience was being kind in a really long line at the grocery store or extending grace to my husband when we faced a disagreement. It wasn't anything out of the ordinary, just a daily part of living. Then it happened. We applied to bring our daughter home for the second time and once again received a resounding *no*. The word *patient* was no longer in my vocabulary. I was devastated, disappointed, angry and weary. Just like the seasons change from summer to fall, the growth I had in the short wait of "summer" automatically started to die in me that day. It was no longer a matter of laying my life down. The cracked foundation of my heart had been broken to pieces as the Lord so kindly began to rebuild a foundation that could never be shaken, but that day "fall" began. There are seasons in your wilderness. Summer is when the heat of the wait hits all at once. It can be uncomfortable, but still look hopeful. Fall is when things start to slowly change, leaving you wondering if your life will ever be the same. Every piece of hope I had up until that point was shattered. It was almost a year after our wait began and seven months after our daughter was born. I had already been through all the emotions and all the facts. We needed a miracle. We knew we needed a miracle from the beginning, but I don't think we knew exactly how desperately we needed one. There were no other options. It was in that moment that God called us to patiently wait.

There are seasons in the waiting, because there is so much that needs done in the process. There was no way I would have been able to address my impatience in the first part of our waiting. There was too much other stuff that needed to be dealt with. Yet, God in His loving kindness saw the parts of my life that needed to look more like Him and He waited to deal with them in the correct time. I didn't have patience. I was angry and hurt in our delay. I wasn't rejoicing in hope, being patient in affliction or being persistent in prayer. I was exhausted, hurt and disappointed. I cried more tears than I thought possible as my mind sank into the reality that we may never be able to take our daughter home. Every piece of faith I had carried to this point vanished the minute we were once again denied.

2 Peter 3:8-9 says,

Dear friends, don't let this one thing escape you: With the Lord one day is like a thousand years, and a thousand years like one day. The Lord does not delay His promise, as some understand delay, but is patient with you, not wanting any to perish but all to come to repentance." HCSB

I lost sight of the big picture in my waiting. How easy it becomes, as we wait through the trials of life, to forget that we're waiting for Jesus to return. We are waiting to spend eternity in heaven with our Father. Our affliction here on earth can feel overwhelming. It can cause us to become so focused on what we see that we forget the big picture. We forget that we have victory through Jesus. Our timeline is not God's timeline. He's not moved or impacted based on the number of days we wait.

If you're still reading this book, you have most likely surrendered your life once again. You chose to pray that God's will would be done. You agreed to giving Him your heart to prune so that you would be able to bear more fruit. But that doesn't mean the days of waiting are easier. It means that you've given Him permission to address issues like patience so that you can be a better reflection of Jesus to the world.

I think about the ways I teach my daughter to be patient. She currently hates to wait as most toddlers do. She doesn't understand why she can't have a cookie before dinner. Let's face it, she doesn't even understand why it takes five seconds of waiting before you can skip the ads on YouTube. She cries, screams, and throws temper tantrums when she doesn't get her way and I laugh. I laugh because I can just see God looking down and smiling over me saying, "Yep, that's what you looked like too." It makes me so thankful that God is so patient with us. His kindness is what draws us to repentance. It is what draws us to Him. If I didn't walk through the process of waiting patiently, I never would have been able to give my daughter, my husband or the world around me a part of the Father's heart that He so longs for us to reflect. He patiently waits for us so that we can patiently wait on Him.

I don't know what miracle you are waiting on, but I do know that your waiting will not be complete without learning the value of patiently waiting. You are not experiencing a delay, but the Lord's loving kindness. Spend some time reading and meditating on 2 Peter 3 today. Ask God to help you see the big picture once again. Ask Him to come into your waiting and strengthen you to rejoice in hope, be patient in affliction, and persistent in prayer. Patiently wait on the Lord. God's promise to you is not delayed.

Day Fourteen
The Danger of Impatience

*Be patient, therefore, brothers, until the coming
of the Lord. See how the farmer waits for the precious
fruit of the earth, being patient about it, until it receives
the early and the late rains. You also, be patient. Establish
your hearts, for the coming of the Lord is at hand.
James 5:7-8 ESV*

Being impatient is not necessarily something
that we think will cause us serious danger. We see it in
relationships when we snap back at a comment we
didn't like. We see it when we cut someone off in the
parking lot. We get impatient for things every single day
and yet, most of the time, our impatience can be made
right with a sincere "I'm sorry." The consequences
never seem like a big deal, but rather just another part
of our crazy busy days. The truth is, we rarely recognize
impatience in the midst of our days. Impatience is
taking the half drank cup of coffee out of the microwave
before the whole minute is up as you chase after your
kids. Impatience is staying irritated with your family for
not cleaning up after themselves for the thousandth
time you've asked. It's staying discontent with where

you are today. It's being in a constant state of restlessness. Impatience is not having things the way we want when we want whenever we want.

Some of you may think you don't struggle with impatience, but I'm willing to guess that you don't have things the way you want 100% of the time. Unfortunately, impatience is so much a part of our daily lives that we don't even recognize it. That right there creates the problem. The danger of impatience sneaks up on us and we never see it coming. I knew I had a problem with patience. Yes, sure I could usually keep my cool with people around me, but the problem was, I hated not being in control. I hated not having the things I wanted when I wanted them. I never saw my need for control as an issue. It's what everyone wants, isn't it? People will tell you that I'm awful at delegating. I would rather be stressed out of my mind and doing everything myself than to release any amount of control I might have. Yet, at the same time my husband will tell you that I'm the most patient person he knows as he watches me teach my daughter to control her emotions. How can it be both ways? How can I possibly long for complete control in one area and be so levelheaded in another?

One of the reasons why I believe God makes us wait is so that we can see what is really in our hearts. It's where our issues of impatience stem from. It becomes dangerous when we don't recognize it. Impatience leads to bitterness, discontentment, anger, unforgiveness, discouragement and a list of other things that can take root in our hearts. These things can sit and linger in our hearts all of our lives. It comes out on random days when we don't expect it too. It causes us to snap at our family when we shouldn't or yell at the person that cut us off in that parking lot. It can cause us to look at God differently. It can cause our view of Him to be unbiblical. It can cause us to be angry at Him or lose hope in the promises He's given us. It can cause us to lose faith. Impatience can cause us to look for a way outside of God's way and outside of His will. This is when it gets dangerous, when all those little acts of impatience cause us to hold unforgiveness or discontentment in our hearts. It makes us search for things outside of God and leads down a road that does not lead to righteousness.

Most likely the impatience you're experiencing in your wait is not because you think you don't have the time to wait for your coffee to heat up. I know it's much bigger than that. But I believe that God is showing you what is in your heart today. I wanted so badly to be with family that first year of my daughter's life. I wanted them to watch her grow. I wanted them to babysit so I could catch up on sleep. I wanted them to be near for family dinners. My heart craved family more than it ever had before. One year turned into two and we were still waiting for our miracle. We missed holidays, birthdays, sick days, and so much more. I was so angry for such a long time. I was discontented with this home we had built because it wasn't where I wanted it to be. Those things flowed out of my heart like rivers. I took it out on God and I'm sure I took it out some days on my husband and daughter too. The loss I felt from not having my family and not being able to be there for them caused the once controlled impatience to rage inside of me. I would scream at God and cry uncontrollable tears as I would ask Him where He went. After we were a year into our wait I began to realize that a lot of that impatience had built up for years and years. Those things had laid dormant in my heart without me ever realizing it. The wait was just what brought them to the surface.

It's through God's kindness that He draws us to repentance. The definition of patience according to Google is "the capacity to accept delay, trouble, or suffering without getting angry or upset." Like me, I'm guessing your waiting has caused impatience to spew out of your heart. Do not let your heart go one more minute without dealing with it. The danger of impatience leads you away from the Father without us even knowing it. It's what the enemy of our souls wants us to walk in. God is doing something in your life right now. He is showing you the areas of your heart that need to be addressed. The areas that are causing things like discontentment, anger, bitterness, discouragement and unforgiveness to take root. He's pruning those areas so that He can heal your heart. When those areas are healed, our hearts overflow with life. God is not having you wait because He's angry at you. He's not having you wait because you messed up or prayed the wrong prayer. God is in the process of pruning, resetting and restoring your heart so that you can run the race that

He has set before you with endurance. God's timing is perfect. Trust Him today to use this time to work in your heart. Rest in knowing that He is holding you in His hands and preparing you for the greatest days of your life.

Spend time today reading the following scriptures. Ask the Lord to show you what areas of your heart are struggling with impatience. Surrender those areas to Him and ask Him to heal you. His kindness will wash over you as you wait patiently for His will and His timing.

Rejoice in hope; be patient in affliction;
be persistent in prayer.
Romans 12:12 HCSB

But if we hope for what we do not see,
we eagerly wait for it with patience.
Romans 8:25 HCSB

Therefore I, the prisoner for the Lord, urge you to walk worthy of the calling you have received, with all humility and gentleness, with patience, accepting one another in love, diligently keeping the unity of the Spirit with the peace that binds us. There is one body and one Spirit - just as you were called to one hope at your calling - one Lord, one faith, one baptism, one God and Father of all, who is above all and through all and in all.
Ephesians 4:1-6 HCSB

Love is patient, love is kind. Love does not envy, is not boastful, is not conceited, does not act improperly, is not selfish, is not provoked, and does not keep a record of wrongs. Love finds no joy in unrighteousness but rejoices in the truth. It bears all things, believes all things, hopes all things, endures all things.
1 Corinthians 13:4-7 HCSB

Therefore, God's chosen ones, holy and loved, put on heartfelt compassion, kindness, humility, gentleness, and patience, accepting one another and forgiving one another if anyone has a complaint against another. Just as the Lord has forgiven you, so you must also forgive.
Colossians 3:12-13 HCSB

Day Fifteen
No Longer A Slave

All those led by God's Spirit are God's sons. For you did not receive a spirit of slavery to fall back into fear, but you received the Spirit of adoption, by whom we cry out, "Abba, Father!" The Spirit Himself testifies together with our spirit that we are God's children, and if children, also heirs - heirs of God and coheirs with Christ - seeing that we suffer with Him so that we may also be glorified with Him.
Romans 8:14-17 HCSB

I was raised in a Christian home, went to church all my life, but I still didn't know what it meant to be God's daughter. I was a people-pleaser bound by an orphan spirit with fears so deep that many aspects of my life were paralyzed. My mind knew God loved me, but my heart always doubted that love. I could win every Bible sword drill, but the Word wasn't breathing over my heart. It's been a decade long process of God slowly chipping away at the fear of abandonment I've carried all my life. When God invites us into the waiting, He is inviting us on a journey of love. It's a journey that allows Him to perfect His love in us. That journey to perfected love is what casts out all fear.

I remember the years leading up to our move abroad. We had begun taking mission teams for a week here and a week there. It fulfilled my heart in so many ways. It was easy to fly in, spend a week in a hotel, eat out, work hard, and fly home seven days later. It was always an adventure. Yet, when God started revealing to us that He wanted us to start planting roots abroad, spend more time there, and say goodbye to the life we knew I faced paralyzing fear and anxiety for years before we left our home in the US. On one trip I brought home parasites that left me so sick I couldn't get out of bed for six months. I never wanted to go back again, but I knew the Lord was calling us there. Each trip after that left me more and more overwhelmed. We didn't speak Spanish. The friends we did have would be 12 hours away from us. We're living out in the middle of the jungle. There was no aspect of our lives at that point that didn't cripple me with fear.

The truth was that fear was just a part of my life. I was a slave to it. It was such a big part of my life that I wouldn't even know how to act when something good was happening. I was always holding my breath waiting for something bad to happen, waiting for the discouragement to sink in. It wasn't something that happened overnight it. It was a lifelong mindset of an orphan spirit. I was adopted when I was a baby. I knew what adoption meant. I knew what it felt like. I knew the love and sacrifice that it took. Yet, there was this spiritual disconnect inside of me that wouldn't let myself be loved as a daughter. God had been working on my heart through the years, but it wasn't until we entered the waiting that He finally told me enough was enough.

The weeks leading up to my daughter's birth was the most terrifying days of my life. It should have been the happiest. The little girl we had been praying for by name was finally going to be in my arms. She was a promise fulfilled. Her life was a miracle. And there I was crying, overwhelmed, and terrified. I had the privilege to walk alongside her birth mother for the last five months of her pregnancy. Barely able to speak her language I spent every day with her, watching her carry this life that she loved but didn't want. She so graciously allowed me to go with her to every doctor's appointment. I sat there not able to understand a word with everyone staring at me and whispering about me. Shaking, unable to breath, I kept putting one foot in front of the other. I didn't know if they would allow me to be in the delivery room or stay in the private clinic after she was born. There were so many other issues going on at the time and I was flat out exhausted. I would hide in our bedroom and cry as often as I could sneak away. It was in that moment that I realized God had begun walking me through every fear I had ever had.

If you had asked me then I would have told you that I knew God loved me and was handling everything, but my heart didn't believe it. My identity was so wrapped up in fear, doubt and abandonment that I didn't have a clue what living like a daughter looked like. I had to walk through every fear I've ever had to understand what being His daughter means. Every aspect of my life had to be tested so that I can stand here today and tell you that God is love. He is trustworthy. His Word is true. Perfect love does cast out fear. I truly believe this process of discovering my true identity in Him could have only been accomplished through the waiting. Everything had to be shaken. Everything had to be tested. It was the time of waiting that allowed me to walk out this identity crisis in a safe place, away from everything I knew and everything I held dear.

In the middle of our waiting, our finances were dead. It looked completely hopeless, and the Holy Spirit told me to go out and buy a guitar. Well, the responsible side of me started freaking out. "How could I do that?" "I don't even know how I'm going to feed my daughter next month." All the thoughts started running through my head. Then I remembered, "I'm the daughter of the King of Kings." So we went to the store, spent money we didn't have, and I came home and worshiped. In that moment my heart was finally at peace, knowing God as my Father. I remembered everything He had walked me through and finally realized that I was no longer a slave. I knew that His love for me and my family was greater than I could ever hope or dream for. I knew I was chosen, wanted and called to be exactly where He had me. It wasn't where I wanted or what I wanted, but I knew in that moment for the first time in a long time that He was there too.

The waiting brings all kinds of fears. It tests your identity as a son or daughter of God. It makes you reexamine what you know and what you truly believe. One thing I know for sure is that this process of waiting perfects God's love inside of us. God is not worried about the time it takes. He doesn't delay or rush. He is patient in molding our lives. He cares so much about our hearts that He is willing to separate us from everything we know so that He can address the places of our lives that don't line up with His will, His plan, His heart and His purposes. You are no longer a slave. You are an heir to the Kingdom of God. Will you walk through your fears with your Father today? Will you follow Him into the deep unknown places of your heart that need to be realigned? Spend today reading 1 John 4:7-19. If your heart is bound in chains today, I pray that God's Spirit would fall on you. Where the Spirit of the Lord is there is freedom. (1 Corinthians 3:17) You are free. You are loved. You are adopted. You are no longer a slave.

Day Sixteen
Healing The Unknown Places of Your Heart

You have turned for me my mourning into dancing;
you have loosed my sackcloth and clothed me with
gladness, that my glory may sing your praise and not be
silent. O LORD my God, I will give thanks to you forever!
Psalms 30:11-12 ESV

     We all have scars. Some are seen by the world and others are only for our own personal viewing. They are a daily reminder of the path we've walked. Each one comes with a story. I can tell you that the scar on my knee was from a bicycle accident when I was about eight years old. When I wear shorts, the whole world can see it. The scar on my eye was from when I got lead paint in my eye on a mission trip to Africa. Only the eye doctor can see that one. The scars on the backs of my ankles are from the first three weeks of us moving overseas. I was so wrapped up in thinking like an orphan at that time that I didn't see the need to buy new shoes before we left behind everything we knew, even though I knew my shoes were on the small side and not the best idea for the terrain we were heading too. I held on to the old shoes for too long, causing these massive scars on both feet.

Every scar has a story. Some of those stories we face victoriously as we remember all we've overcome. The other ones are a constant reminder of the pain, trials and tears we've cried along the way. The scars can be a traumatic form of stress or our greatest battle story. But even greater than the physical scars we carry are the ones that are held in our hearts. The places no one sees. The scars that are sometimes even unknown to us. When I was living in the jungle, I got dengue fever. It was the most physically painful thing I've ever been through. You can still, to this day, play connect the dots from one mosquito bite to the next, but even that greatest pain didn't compare to the scars on my heart in my waiting.

When we wait on the Lord a lot of things happen. Emotions come to the surface. Time seems to stop. The silence can feel overwhelming. It's in this new reality where we start to see what we look like inside and out. I realized my body had scars I never knew I had. Even more so, I realized the scars my heart was carrying. Scars I never knew existed. The waiting can leave us feeling as if we're all alone. It can feel as if God turned His back on us or silently walked away. The loneliness and disappointment can slowly start to open those scars back up, making us feel hopeless for any kind of relief. How often we forget the Truth when the weight of the world is on our shoulders.

It's during the waiting when God, in His kindness, allows us to feel all our emotions. We can't realize the depth of His power to heal until we realize the unknown places of our heart that need Him. It's painful to feel weak with our scars on display. It's easy to get angry and throw our fists up in the air, but in our weakness, His power is made perfect. It's seeing the broken places of our lives on display that brings us to surrender. I remember many nights on my knees crying out for God to fix things. Of course, I was asking Him to fix them the way I wanted them to be fixed. Yet, in His kindness He showed me that what I needed was for Him to heal my heart.

What's inside our heart matters. It's out of our heart that our mouth speaks. (Luke 6:45) From our hearts flow the springs of life. (Proverbs 4:23) We put so much time and effort into placing band-aids over our hearts. We try to cover them with busyness, productivity and random stuff. Instead of letting God heal our hearts, we go on for years, leaking dangerous emotions into the world around us. We use band-aids in hopes that our scars will disappear. We pretend they aren't there. The band-aids seems to last until the waiting season begins. They last until life slows down and you're sitting in the wilderness all alone. It's then that the waiting shows you what's truly in your heart.

Psalms 30 speaks about joy coming in the morning. Today, I want to encourage you that the morning does come. You may feel like you're waiting through a whole bunch of long nights, but it's not forever. The Lord will heal you. It's what He is longing to do right now. He cares so much about your heart that He was willing to pull you away to do nothing more than to be with Him. I don't know why or what you're waiting for right now. Maybe you're waiting for a job, waiting to be healed from a disease, or waiting for reconciliation in your family. Maybe you are waiting for a promotion, waiting for a promise or like my family, waiting for a miraculous way home. The reason doesn't matter as to why you're on this journey of waiting. What matters is what you're going to do with it.

Will you allow God to heal the unknown places of your heart? He wants to heal every scar. He wants your heart to be whole, not broken. He will turn your mourning into dancing. This is who He is and it's what He does. In His loving kindness, He has brought you to this place so that you can be full, not empty so that you can experience all that Jesus died to give you. You don't have to live with the traumatic memories of yesterday any longer. You don't have to look down and see your scars bleeding every day. Will you invite the Holy Spirit to heal your heart? Take time today to sit at Jesus' feet and read Psalm 30. Nothing is impossible for God. There is no scar too deep for Him to heal. You will dance for joy today as the unknown places of your heart experience the unending love of the Father. There is joy for you to find today on this journey of heart healing. May your heart become whole as you seek the Father.

Day Seventeen
The Beauty Of Tears

"Those who sow in tears shall reap in shouts of joy!
Psalms 126:5 HCSB

After we realized for the first time that God's plan was not our plan and we weren't going home how or when we thought we would, we started to panic. We were in a foreign city, living in a hotel, with a newborn. It wasn't quite how I pictured it. I had so much faith at the beginning of our journey. There was not a doubt in my mind that God was going to bring us home as a family of three to our homeland and our family. Then issue after issue left us stuck in what felt like a prison. We finally found a small apartment that was modern and felt closer to home than any other place we had lived in. It wasn't what I wanted, but for the first time it felt like we were safe.

We lived in that little apartment for five months. It was near a bike trail where we could go for walks every day. It overlooked a busy intersection that always had some type of entertainment going on in the streets day and night. It was loud but felt a million miles away from the world. I would sit on the floor and overlook the traffic after my husband and daughter had fallen asleep. Most nights there was nothing I could do to keep the tears from soaking the floor beneath me. I didn't understand why God didn't do the miracle I thought He would do. I would sit in the same spot night after night unable to pray, to think, and unable to process any of the difficult things that were happening in our life every day. We didn't know where to go, what to do next, or most importantly what God was saying to us during those months. All I could do was sit there and cry night after night. There were no words that I could put together.

The days went on and eventually so did our scenery, but the tears wouldn't seem to stop. I longed for things to be "normal", to have family nearby, to have a rocking chair that I could rock my baby girl to sleep in. I longed for God to do the miracle He told me He was going to do. But those things never came. I wasted so many days that should have been full of joy. The little girl I prayed for by name was finally in my arms, but I could not get over the fact that we had entered the waiting.

Tears are a part of life. Most often we view them as an outlet for pain, grief and disappointment. These seasons happen for all of us at one point or another. The wilderness always tends to draw the tears out. We try to hide them and push the emotions away. But what if the tears are part of the miracle? One of the most quoted scriptures in the Bible is John 11:35. It says, *"Jesus wept."* We hear it a lot in Christian circles because it's the shortest verse in the Bible, but also because we can all relate. What goes unnoticed are the verses around it. John 11:28-37 talks about the story of Lazarus. At this point Lazarus had already been in the tomb for four days. Verse 32 says,

"When Mary came to where Jesus was and saw Him, she fell at His feet and told Him, 'Lord, if You had been here, my brother would not have died!'" HCSB

Jesus was overcome with anger and deeply moved when He saw Mary crying. It was this emotion that led Him to weep. It was also His tears that brought the miracle. Jesus, the Son of God, could have immediately gone to Lazarus when He got the word that He was sick. He could have healed Lazarus right then and there. Yet, John 11:6 tells us,

"So when He heard that He was sick, He stayed two more days in the place where He was." HCSB

He waited. This leads us to ask questions. Why did He wait? What was He doing while He waited? It probably leads us to the exact same questions you've asked in your time of waiting. Jesus knew exactly what was going on with Lazarus. John 11:4 says,

"When Jesus heard it, He said, 'This sickness will not end in death but is for the glory of God, so that the Son of God may be glorified through it." HCSB

He knew exactly what was happening every step of the way. Yet, He waited. Then He cried.

I used to think obedience was easy for me. I had no problem following Jesus into the unknown. Then He led me into a jungle and asked me to wait. It was then that the tears began to flow. I never could have imagined the sacrifice that it would take to follow Jesus. For so long I thought that the tears were a picture of my lack of faith. I was ashamed of them. I wanted to be stronger. I wanted to proclaim the goodness of God. I wanted Him to be glorified through me. How could waiting be a part of God's plan? If He can do all things, why does He choose to wait? Why does He call us to wait? I always think back to those nights I sat on the floor looking over the traffic, crying. The tears had been holding so many emotions inside. I couldn't process anything that was happening to the point where I couldn't hear what the Holy Spirit was saying to me during that time. The grief was too heavy. The confusion, exhaustion, and anger were too much for me to bear. So, I sat, and I cried.

It was the tears that brought the miracle. It wasn't the miracle that I was praying for or longing for. It was the miracle that God knew I needed. My heart's desire was to glorify Him, but in order to do that I needed to know His heart. If my heart was so cluttered with the world, how was I supposed to hear the Holy Spirit? 1 Corinthians 2:10-12 says,

"Now God has revealed these things to us by the Spirit, for the Spirit searches everything, even the depths of God. For who among men knows the thoughts of a man except the spirit of the man that is in him? In the same way, no one knows the thoughts of God except the Spirit of God. Now we have not received the spirit of the world, but the Spirit who comes from God so that we may

understand what has been freely given to us by God."
HCSB

In God's loving kindness He let me feel. Though I didn't recognize it at the time He gave me a safe place where I could rest, cry, and process so that I could hear His voice once again. The waiting is a safe place for you to heal. Our tears remind us of our daily need for Jesus. Our weakness shows just how powerful God is. If tears have been a part of your life lately I encourage you to look past the pain and find the beauty. God is there with you. He is letting you feel everything you need to so that He can start rebuilding on a heart that is fully healed. Read the story of Lazarus in John 11 today. The miracle is found in the beauty of your tears.

Day Eighteen
Awakening LOVE

*For God loved the world in this way: He gave
His One and Only Son, so that everyone who
believes in Him will not perish but have eternal life.
John 3:16 HCSB*

I never realized the things that were part of my identity until I walked through the waiting. It was all based on things I could control, things that made me feel safe and loved and things based on my fears and insecurities. I had loved Jesus since I was little, but no part of my perceived identity was grounded on His word or His truth. I knew all of the Sunday school answers but didn't know how to live as a daughter. The longer our waiting continued, the more intense the dismantling of my identity became. When everything was left outside my control, my fears and insecurities were left screaming in my face. It wasn't just that I didn't know who God said I was, I realized that I didn't know who God said *He* was. After I gave my heart to Jesus, time went on. My faith grew. I saw incredible miracles. I heard and believed incredible testimonies. At the same time, the darkness of the world, broken people and life slowly crept in without me ever noticing it. All the lies of the enemy started getting mixed with the Truth of Jesus and slowly, scales formed over my eyes. My broken identity left me busy, but unproductive, as I searched to fill the voids. It left me tired and drained every day. I had to constantly be doing something to prove something to God. I had to stay busy so that I could earn His love. Somehow, I began thinking that I had to do things to even keep His love. It wasn't what I was taught when I first started following Jesus. I knew the Bible. It was only the lies of the enemy that I allowed to take hold, transformed my thinking.

It wasn't until we were in the middle of the waiting that I realized I didn't know the God of the Bible anymore. My identity was so misplaced that I didn't even know where to begin. It's easy to say that your foundation is firm when everything is going your way. It's in the waiting that God shows you the areas of your heart that are not aligned with Him. Not only did our waiting leave us far away from anyone we knew, it also left us in a place we didn't even speak the same language. No part of our lives was the same after God invited us into the wilderness. So, we clung to what we knew ourselves to be. As I look back, I see God's kindness all over those early days. I see Him caring so much about us that He would pull us away into this safe place where we could do nothing more than get to know His heart. It didn't feel like His kindness during those days though. Every day felt heavy. Every day left me feeling like a failure. Every day felt like I was drowning.

I would love to tell you that God one day immediately awakened me to His love, but that wasn't how it happened. It took days, months and even years for God to walk me through the process of waiting before I was awakened to His love. At one point, through it all, He awakened me. He took me back to the beginning, stripped me of everything I knew and carefully began to rebuild my identity. He took me back to creation and walked me through His sacrifice of Jesus awakening my heart to a life of being His daughter, His beloved.

It reminds me of the story of Paul's conversion in Acts 9:1-19. Saul, later known as Paul, hated Christians. He persecuted them and murdered them. He was not the picture of a son. Yet, God had chosen him. Verse 15 says,

"Go, for he is a chosen instrument of mine to carry my name before the Gentiles and kings and the children of Israel." ESV

In one moment on the road to Damascus, a light from heaven shone around him and he heard a voice calling to him asking why he was persecuting Jesus. Can you imagine the identity issues Saul was facing? One day he was killing Christians and the next he was being filled with the Holy Spirit and proclaiming Jesus as the Son of God in the synagogues. When Jesus approached him on the road that day, he became blind, much like the spiritual life he had been living, but the Lord, in His kindness, sent Ananias to lay hands on him. Verses 18 and 19 say,

"And immediately something like scales fell from his eyes, and he regained his sight. Then he rose and was baptized; and taking food, he was strengthened." ESV

You most likely have not been persecuting Christians, but I'm guessing that your time of waiting has brought you to question who you are. It may feel like you're even questioning who God is. Your questions may even leave you feeling lifeless and without hope. But I can assure you that God is restoring your life. In His kindness, He has removed the distractions so that you can address the questions in your heart. In His kindness, He is reintroducing Himself to you so that you can know the God of the Bible. He doesn't want you to only know the things you've been taught, or the lessons life has given you. He wants you to know *Him*. From there, He wants you to know who you are in Him, as His son or daughter. John 3:16 says,

"God so loved the world that He gave His only Son, that whoever believes in him should not perish but have eternal life." ESV

He loves you so much that He gave everything so that you could be restored to Him.

Sometimes we get so caught up in what we see today that we lose sight of the big picture. I had loved Jesus since I was little. I knew that I was a daughter of God, yet I didn't know how to live out those truths. I didn't know how they applied to my life when everything else was taken away. Like Saul, I had scales over my eyes, but when I surrendered to the wait and endured the process God had laid before me, I was then awakened to His love. The truth was separated from the lies and He began to sharpen me like a sword (Isaiah 49:2) so that I could become all He created me to be. He wanted me to be an over-comer so that I could, once again, wear His armor and be a light to the nations.

God is awakening you to His love today. You may have scales over your eyes and your heart may be tired, but God has chosen you. He has chosen you for such a time as this and He is using your waiting to strengthen you for His glory. I remember the first time I felt like my spirit was awakened. I felt like I could breathe for the very first time. I was no longer trying to convince myself of His love. I could actually feel it in my veins. Today is that day for you. Will you ask the Holy Spirit to awaken you? Will you sit in the stillness and wait for the love of God to wash over you. The war you've been waging has been over your identity. The enemy of your soul knows that when you awaken to the love of God, to your identity in Christ, that it is game over for him. I pray that you would be filled with the Holy Spirit, that you would know who God is, and who you are in Him. Spend time reading Acts 9 today. Rest in the love of God as He awakens your heart to breathe again.

Day Nineteen
The Time In Between

So teach us to number our days
that we may get a heart of wisdom.
Psalms 90:12 ESV

I could see the promise land before the waiting began. The Lord was so kind to give me dreams and visions about what life looked like on the other side. It was those prophetic words and dreams the Lord placed in my heart that kept me clinging to hope when my life felt like it was falling apart. I saw the wait begin in one moment. I knew what was coming after. It was the days in between that left me shaken to the core. How could I speed up time? How could I fix what was outside of my control? Isn't there something I should be doing that could make everything right? So many questions I would ask myself. It left me feeling like a failure every single day as I tried so desperately to leave the waiting. Days, weeks, months, and years went by before I felt the Holy Spirit reminding me to number my days. As I looked back, I realized that every day that felt unending, in all reality, passed by too quickly. I wasn't holding a sweet little baby in my arms; I was chasing after a toddler. Those days that I had wished away were actually gone. I spent so many days in heartache that I missed all the joy that went with them.

It's the time in between the start and the finish that truly matters. It's the days we take for granted and the days we wish away that are valuable. It's the process of waiting that frees us, heals us and restores us. It's the time in between where God does His best work in us. Yet, those are the days we don't want. Those are the days we try to run and hide from. The promise land is great. It's the gift. But God will do everything He needs to do inside of us first, so that we can fully receive all He wants to give us. It's easy to play the victim card in the waiting. It's easier to get angry and blame God for circumstances instead of allowing Him to heal and restore us. It's easy to just wish the hard days away, but Psalms 90:12 reminds us to number our days. Tomorrow is not promised. If we keep wishing away our todays, when will we ever be able to enjoy the life we've been given?

When I think about the time in between, it reminds me of the time between the death and resurrection of Jesus. I cannot imagine the silence Jesus' followers felt in their hearts. How empty their hearts must have felt when the One they loved was crucified. Even the ones with the greatest faith had to be questioning what was happening. They knew Jesus would resurrect, but how devastating that moment must have felt. The time in between the death and resurrection of Jesus must have felt like an eternity. Oh, the grief, confusion, and despair they must have felt. Yet, it was that time that fulfilled the scriptures. It was that time that proved Jesus was the Son of God. It was that time that brought salvation to the world.

I was always good at playing the victim in my mind during the time in between. I thought I deserved, this or that, because I was stuck in a place I didn't want to be. I thought I was allowed to stay angry or depressed because God wasn't giving me what I wanted and then He told me to remember that my days were numbered. It was then that I awoke and realized how many days I'd missed. I was going through the motions, watching my daughter grow up before my eyes and yet I was missing all of it. I wasn't cherishing the days, the milestones, or any of the joy those days brought simply because it wasn't how I wanted to be doing it. My victim mentality was keeping me in bondage. I missed everything God was doing during that time. It wasn't until He asked me to remember my days that I finally started to experience joy again. I started looking back through pictures to remind myself of everything God had done along the way. There was so many miracles and moments of joy that I had overlooked, because I wasn't looking for the thing He was doing. I was holding on to the ways I wanted Him to operate. I put God in a box thinking that His will looked a specific way. It left me to realize the new thing He was doing in my heart and life didn't even slightly resemble what I was used to. I can't imagine the disciples had a clear picture of the time in between Jesus' death and resurrection either.

They probably had a picture in their head of the exact way He would show up after His resurrection or maybe through all the grief they forgot He was coming back. Thomas didn't even believe the other disciples when they told him they had seen Jesus. (John 20:24-29) Yet it didn't change God's plan.

The time in between the start of your wait and the promise land is not a time to waste. Your days are numbered, and each day is a gift. Will you find the joy in today or will you wish it away? Will you surrender to the process God has laid before you? The promise land will come, but the time in between is where the miracles happen. Ask the Holy Spirit to help you number your days. Ask for your heart to be open to whatever God wants to do. Ask Him to awaken your heart so that you can see and hear Him correctly. You do not want to miss the new thing He is doing in your heart and life. There is so much joy available for you, today. It may be hard to see, but it is there. I pray that the presence of God would fill your heart. I pray that you would see and discern the new ways God is revealing Himself to you. You are not a victim. You are a child of God walking through the journey of waiting. There is purpose in the time in between. The miracles you have been asking for are actually happening, today. Read the story of the death and resurrection of Jesus in John 19 and 20 today. Take communion and remember what has already been done for you. He is good and He is faithful in every minute of your life. God doesn't waste anything. Look for the joy. Today is a gift. You need to unwrap and receive it.

Day Twenty
Child of God

But to all who did receive Him, He gave them the
right to be children of God, to those who believe in
His name, who were born, not of blood, or of the will
of the flesh, or of the will of man, but of God.
John 1:12 ESV

How differently things become when God doesn't
show up how or when we want Him to. The family
member wasn't healed like you thought they would be.
The debt left you filing for bankruptcy. The school didn't
accept your application. Justice wasn't delivered how
you thought it should be. All the things of life can leave
us with questions that lead to more questions. The
longer they go unanswered, the more it causes us to
search for the truth and cling to what has always been.
Unanswered prayers and times of waiting can bring out
the greatest crisis of faith we'll ever experience. Some
people decide to base their view of God on whether life
is unfolding how they want it to. Others dive in to
surrender, asking God to reveal the Truth even when it

hurts. Many people run from God when life gets hard. Some people walk away completely.

The waiting causes us to look at God differently. It causes us to question His nature and His character. It causes us to question what we were taught and search for answers. This is one of the reasons why I believe God asks us to wait. It's through the questions where we truly search to discover who He is. It's in the waiting where we turn back to the Bible. When life is going well, and everything feels peaceful it's easy to put our pursuit of God on autopilot. It's comfortable. We go to church on Sunday. We meet up for small group in the middle of the week. We check the boxes on our Bible app and life is great. But it's in the waiting, in the moments where breathing seems difficult where we fall on our faces and cry out for Him.

I remember a conference I attended several years ago. I couldn't tell you the name of the speaker, yet I can still hear the words she spoke. It was the first time I ever heard anyone talk about sonship. I'm sure I heard it a million times growing up in church, but it was then that my spirit actually heard it. Just the word, sonship, struck my heart. Even though I'd known Jesus from the time I was a little girl, it was in that moment that God started taking me on this journey of knowing Him as Father. After the excitement of this revelation had faded, the autopilot began. Life was hard at times, but great. I was introduced to God as my Father and saw Him provide for my family and produce miracle after miracle in our ministry. Then, God said wait and everything I believed about Him as my Father caused all these doubts, fears and insecurities to rise up out of nowhere. Where did He go? How can God still be good with this happening? Has He abandoned us? Is He mad at us? What are we doing wrong? There were so many questions swirling around in my heart that caused me to question everything I knew about God.

The questions can cause a lot of shame and guilt. They reveal wrong belief systems. They illuminate areas of doubt. They show us how we sometimes walk in fear instead of love. The questions are not bad. They actually show us what we really believe. Sometimes, asking the questions or writing them down in a journal can be very helpful in processing the pain and emotional roller coaster of waiting.

At the end of the day, it is what you do with your questions that matters. Is your view of God the same no matter what the circumstances are around you, or does your view of God change based on whether things are going good or going bad?

God is unchanging. He is the same yesterday, today, and forever. The God of the Bible that you know when things are going your way is the same God of the Bible that exists on your worst days. He doesn't change, but your emotions do. He doesn't change, but your circumstances do. It is one thing to believe in your mind that God is who He says He is. It is another thing to believe it in your heart. John 1:12 tells us that to those who receive Him and believe in His name have the right to become children of God. He introduced me to Himself as Father before I entered the waiting, yet it was during all the questioning where my heart was able to fully believe that I was His child.

You can memorize all the right scriptures and know all the worship songs, but if your heart doesn't know how to worship through every season of life, your heart will struggle to believe God is who He says He is. It is only in knowing *who God is* that we can know *who we are*, as His children. The waiting also gives us a choice to either live out our lives, completely depending on Him, or to become independent and struggle every day. To walk away from the world, lay down our lives and depend on God to sustain us will eventually reveal every area of weakness we have. It is through our weaknesses that we can see and understand the magnitude of the sacrifices Jesus made so that we could be children of God. It's impossible to have a revelation of our need and experience any kind of dependence on God as Father when our relationship with Him is on autopilot. It's the waiting and the time of questioning, where God slowly removes all of the lies, doubts and fears we carry that allows us to understand what it means to call Him our Father. It's in these times that God will remind us of who He is, how He loves us and why we love Him. It's in this place where He establishes our identity as His sons and daughters.

It's okay to ask all the questions, but when you ask make sure you are taking the time to sit and listen. God will answer the deepest questions of your heart. He will sift the lies from the truth. He will reveal your identity as His child. He will restore what's been lost and bring you to a new understanding of His love. The real question is will you surrender to this process? You will step out of this season far better equipped to worship God through every situation, because you will *know* God. You will know Him in ways you never would have known Him if it wasn't for your time in the wilderness. He is inviting you to walk with Him today. Your greatest weapon against the enemy is knowing who you are as a child of God. Will you allow God to transform your mind, answer your questions and establish His heart in your life? Read Romans 8 today. Remember the sacrifice of Jesus and praise Him for the opportunity we have been given to receive the spirit of adoption as coheirs with Christ!

Winter

Make me to know your ways, O LORD; teach me your paths. Lead me in your truth and teach me, for you are the God of my Salvation; for you I wait all the day long.
Psalms 25:4-5 ESV

Day Twenty-One
Reestablishing Trust

When I am afraid, I put my trust in you.
In God, whose word I praise, in God I trust;
I shall not be afraid. What can flesh do to me?
Psalms 56:3-4 ESV

Trust is something that is earned in relationships. It can take years to form a bond that produces trust. It can take seconds to lose that trust. Trust is something that needs a firm foundation to thrive on. As humans, we tend to not give trust freely. It's something that comes with a lot of work and a lot of time. Trust is something that must be protected and cared for. We put our trust in a lot of things every day without really thinking about it. We trust the electric company to keep the power on. We trust the bank to keep our money safe. We trust our neighbors to keep an eye on our home when we're away. We trust our pastors with leading our church. We trust the security guards at the mall to keep us safe. When trust is broken, the damage it does can produce shame, guilt, disappointment and so many other negative emotions. Sometimes that loss of trust is from miscommunication. Sometimes it is from sin in our hearts. Other times it's simply from not knowing the person or thing we've put our trust in.

Regardless of who or what you place your trust in there comes a day when that trust is tested. When God says wait, we can be sure that our trust in Him or our distrust in Him will be addressed. The silence that comes with the wait reveals how our hearts feel about God and how much we truly trust Him. If you would have asked me before our waiting began if I trusted in Jesus, I would have said absolutely yes. It wasn't until the wait when I realized that, although I trust in Jesus for my salvation, I wasn't actually sure I trusted Him with my life, here and now. I knew Proverbs 3:5-6 since I was little.

"Trust in the LORD with all your heart, and do not rely on your own understanding; think about Him in all your ways, and He will guide you on the right paths." HCSB

It's one thing to know what the Bible says, but it's a completely different thing to live it and believe it in your heart.

The Lord had proven His faithfulness over and over to me for so many years. He answered prayers. He did miracles. He spoke to me in specific ways. I knew what His presence felt like. Yet, it's clear now that my trust was only partial. Although it felt deep at the time, my trust in Jesus was truly shallow. It was based solely on the box I had put Him in. Several years before God invited us to wait on Him, I started praying that I would experience His fullness. I wanted to know all of Him. I wanted to receive everything He had for me. Then we entered the waiting and life got still. The silence was uncomfortable and overwhelming. My mind didn't know how to release the busyness of my mind to the quietness of my days. I would search for things to keep my hands busy while my heart slowly, day by day, lost trust in the One I loved. I clung to Jesus every day, but as things started to turn from one disappointment to another, my shallow trust started disappearing. I would tell myself and everyone around me that I trusted God, but my heart was not confident that He would actually show up. I knew He could, but most days I wasn't sure if He would.

After God shook the summer and fall seasons of the waiting off my life a new season began when He started reestablishing a deeper level of trust. He finally had a clean slate to work with. I had surrendered to the process. I was ready for Him to do whatever He wanted to do, however He wanted to do it. He knew I wanted to trust Him, but He also knew I needed some serious work in that department. So, He quietly started making His way back in. With no dishwashers in the jungle, I would wash dishes multiple times a day. It was a time I grew to love, because it was in those moments where He would talk to me the most. I could feel His presence again. All the junk and distractions that had piled up on me for years and years was finally cleared out and He began to ever so kindly share His heart with me again. The laws of religion that I had fallen into were all broken off of me as our relationship started to mend and trust started to reform. It wasn't something that happened overnight. It was only one part of the process of waiting. In order to receive His fullness, I had to let go of my preconceived ideas of how He operated. I had to remember He was limitless and all powerful. He can do whatever He wants, however He wants. All He needs from us is trust and surrender.

Even after trust was restored the walls of protection, I had placed around my heart were difficult to take down. I had started trusting God again but was not confident that He would come. I knew He *could*. The question that was always in the back of my mind was, *would He?* For a while we were able to make individual trips back and forth to the US to restock our supplies, but those days started to become few and far between. It was when our vitamins started getting low in the middle of a pandemic that the Holy Spirit convicted me. If I could trust God with my soul, why couldn't I trust Him to keep us healthy even after the vitamins ran out? I had placed so much trust in the things we had that my confident trust in Him was nothing more than words on a page. After years of waiting and walking out the process I was still struggling to receive His love. The fear of more disappointment and the fear of lack caused my heart to push Him away instead of allowing Him to come in all His fullness.

This process is about so much more than your promise. The time is not being wasted. God is working in your heart to clear out the junk so that you can confidently trust in who He is. You can't receive His love without it. You also can't *give* His love without it. God wants to be able to trust you with His heart. He can't do that until you trust Him with yours. Sometimes I think we skip steps. We go from being saved to saving others. It's a great thing, but often times we skip the process of heart healing. This leads to burn out, wrong mindsets, and leaves us teaching things based on what we know and feel instead of the Truth. This journey of waiting is so that God can realign your heart with His. It's important. These days are not meant to be skipped or wished away. They are meant for you to heal so that you can continue running the race set before you. They are used for pruning so you can actually *bear more fruit.* Spend some time writing down the areas that you don't confidently trust God with. Be honest. He already knows. Ask Him to come and do what only He can do in your heart today. Ask Him to help you trust Him more. Read Proverbs 3:5, Psalms 56:3-4, Jeremiah 29:11, 1 John 4:18, Isaiah 26:3-4 and Psalm 37:5 today. Your trust in Jesus is being reestablished today. It's a new day. Rejoice! As the old hymn goes:

> *Tis so sweet to trust in Jesus*
> *Just to take Him at His Word*
> *Just to rest upon His promise*
> *Just to know, 'Thus saith the Lord!*
> *Jesus, Jesus, how I trust Him!*
> *How I've proved Him o'er and o'er*
> *Jesus, Jesus, precious Jesus!*
> *Oh, for grace to trust Him more!*

May you confidently rest in Jesus today as you are reunited with your First Love.

Day Twenty-Two
The Birthing Pains

But I am afflicted and in pain; let your salvation,
O God, set me on high! I will praise the name of God
with a song; I will magnify him with thanksgiving.
Psalm 69:29-30 ESV

    I personally have never given birth, but I have watched multiple women bring life into this world. I don't think anyone can say labor is easy or pain free. While I cannot relate to the physical pains of childbirth, I felt so much pain as I watched my daughter's birth mother bring my daughter into this world. I was so sure that she was going to arrive early. I was actually positive. I was so positive that I stopped sleeping weeks before her due date so that I could be ready at a minute's notice. Her due date came and went and still no baby in my arms. With every passing day my heart was bound by fear, wondering if her birth mother would change her mind and decide to keep the little miracle inside her womb. I couldn't eat and couldn't sleep. I was anxious, full of fear and left waiting. Waiting and more waiting. I had no idea that this waiting would lead us into a much deeper and intense season of waiting. Finally, the day came. We went to the clinic only to be sent on another long walk around the park. With every labor pain she felt, my heart experienced a deeper level of pain. I was so anxious, I couldn't breathe. My heart grieved for the loss she was feeling and the trauma she endured to birth my miracle baby. My heart grieved that I wasn't the one carrying this precious life inside of me. I had pain from the fear of the days ahead and of all the unknowns that lay before me. It was if the birthing pains would hit in waves. One minute I was excited with anticipation that I would soon hold my baby in my arms. The next minute, I was overwhelmed by pain. Emotional, mental, spiritual, and even physical pain as my emotions started overflowing through vomiting and migraines. I actually could not keep any food or water in my body for the first two weeks of my daughter's life. Those were my birthing pains. Every part of me was impacted by the waves of emotion that birthing pains bring.

If you've given birth, you know the pain of labor. You know all about the physical birthing pains. Not everyone is familiar with the physical pain of labor, but one thing we all can understand and have experienced at one time or another is waves of pain. Whether it was emotional, physical, mental, or spiritual I imagine you can picture a time in your life where you felt hit by those unrelenting waves. One moment the pain hits hard as if you were sitting on the sand at the beach and blindsided by a strong wave. The next moment there may be a moment of peace where you're sitting on the same sand but feel the warmth of the sun shining down on you as the water pulls off the shore. These birthing pains, or waves of pain, come in seasons but can catch us off guard even more so during times of waiting.

When we wait, we're almost forced to dwell in our emotions. We find out what is truly in our hearts when things slow down. When we wait, we can no longer hide behind busyness or the constant demands of the world. We can no longer hide behind the walls we've consciously and subconsciously placed around our hearts. So, there we sit on the beach of waiting. Full of faith and strength in the beginning, feeling the warm sun fill us with fresh air. We breathe deeply and then, out of nowhere comes the anger. It crashes over us out of nowhere. You probably didn't even know you had anger in your heart. Then, a second wave hits you before you can even recover from the first one. Maybe this wave is filled with grief. It's emotionally and mentally exhausting, being hit by the emotional waves of waiting. Soon after you are hit with two waves or birthing pains there's a calm, a peace that only Jesus can give. The areas of your heart that needed healing have been addressed and you're able to breathe again. Days, weeks, maybe even months go by yet you find yourself still waiting, still needing breakthrough, still praying for a miracle. All of a sudden, another wave hits, another pain shoots deep inside your heart. And the cycle continues.

Does this sound familiar? A couple good days and then more grief. A couple good weeks then more anger.

A couple months and then another trauma. It's the birthing pains of waiting. It may not seem like it when you're going through these waves, but the birthing pains are good news! Just as physical birthing pains lead to a beautiful little baby, your waiting pains are leading you to victory! They are preparing your heart and mind to receive the miracle you've been praying for. Sometimes these hard winter seasons are necessary for us to receive the answers to the prayers we've been praying. The Lord is more concerned about your heart than the number of days you've been waiting. In His loving kindness, He will never rush to answer us. Whether you've been waiting a month or even years, the Lord is patient with us to make sure we are healed, whole and prepared to receive what we're waiting for. The Lord does His greatest work when we're waiting. When we create the time to sit with our emotions, thoughts, and pain and invite Jesus in to heal us of our deepest wounds is when we begin seeing those labor pains ending and a new life beginning.

What can we do when we feel the birthing pains of life? It's easy to run away from those emotions. It's easy to bury them deep inside. But, if you're waiting on something, that pain might be your invitation into Joy. Will you let the waves of waiting wash over you? Will you let the Lord heal the areas of your heart that need to be whole? Psalm 69:29-30 says,

"But I am afflicted and in pain; let your salvation, O God, set me on high! I will praise the name of God with a song; I will magnify him with thanksgiving." ESV

Jesus is with you right now. He knows your every hurt, your every trauma, your every fear. He loves you too much to let you go another day with a broken heart. Will you trust Him, as you are being bombarded with waiting pains, to take your life and make something beautiful? Rejoice that Jesus meets us in our brokenness and resurrects our lives. He is healing areas of your heart that you didn't even know needed healing. He's healing trauma that you have stuffed so deep down inside that you forgotten all the details.

Your waiting pains are ending. Your joy is coming. Rejoice for the Lord is setting you on high. Praise Him. Magnify Him with thanksgiving. Your season of waiting is transforming you in ways you could never even imagine.

"For his anger is but for a moment, and his favor is for a lifetime. Weeping may tarry for the night, but joy comes with the morning."
Psalm 30:5 ESV

Day Twenty-Three
Surrendering Your Timetable

A man's heart plans his way,
but the LORD determines his steps.
Proverbs 16:9 HCSB

Isn't it funny how even from a young age we hate to wait. We're in a time where we can get everything we want or need instantly. We have microwaves to make our food. The internet to search for every answer. We can download any song known to man within seconds. We can skip the commercials on every streaming service. Our life is fast and getting faster by the day. If you've ever been to Disney, you have probably bought the "Fast Pass" once or twice. We're willing to spend a ridiculous amount of extra money just so we can skip the line on the amusement park ride that we already paid to ride. While sometimes choosing to skip the line makes sense, it has left us in a world that is unable to cope when the waiting begins. We've become parents that answer instantly just to avoid the meltdowns. We've become bound by fear when the one we love doesn't answer the phone call or text message within five minutes. We get annoyed and angry at people in the grocery store when the line is too long, or the cashier is too slow. We've planned our lives in so much detail that we operate best when waiting is nonexistent.

From a young age most people set a plan in place. By this age I'll graduate. By this year I'll be married. By this time, I'll have children. By this age I'll retire. We plan and prepare our steps usually in great detail. Yet, waiting never seems to make the list. So, what do we do when our plans and timetables get shaken? We're so used to the instantaneous life. How do we move forward when our plans are no longer an option? Surrender sounds easy until our lives are out of our own hands.

When the Lord led us into waiting, we had a plan. Sure, we'll have to wait a little while. But we had all the prophetic words spoken over us. We had all the prayer warriors. We had peace. We were ready to walk through the process of bringing our daughter home. Those three weeks of planned waiting turned into three years and counting. We would start one process only to have every door closed. Then another and another. Only to be met with disappointment, anger, confusion, and grief. "But Lord!" our hearts would cry. "We know you led us here. We know we're walking in obedience. We know you confirmed this in us." Our timeline caused so much pain. Our timeline caused so much doubt. Our timeline caused so much fear and anxiety. Our timeline. We wanted to rush the process. We wanted to instantaneously walk into the promise land. But God in

His loving kindness saw our weaknesses. He saw our brokenness. He saw our exhaustion. He saw the areas of our heart that needed Him. He saw our family. He saw me. In His loving kindness, He walked us through the pain caused by our own plans, and He directed our steps. I cannot imagine what life would look like if God would have given us our miracles when we wanted them. Because now, looking back, I can see all the areas He's healed, restored, redeemed and set free through this plan that wasn't our own. At some point I laid down my timetable. I surrendered it at the feet of Jesus. It didn't physically change anything, but it changed everything inside of me. I finally realized how many days I wasted. I realized how much joy I had missed. My eyes were opened to all the things I took for granted. It led me to repentance for hating this season of life that seemed so hard and so painful. It was in my surrender that I realized that the whole time I was struggling, the Lord was inviting me to receive His joy.

It reminds me of the story of Joseph. (Genesis 37-50) Joseph knew after receiving a dream from the Lord that one day his brothers would be bowing down to him, yet never in a million years would Joseph imagine that he would walk through the wilderness like he did. His own brothers sold him into slavery. He was in prison. He was accused and betrayed. He was far away from his family. Then miraculously, he was put in charge of Egypt where his brothers ended up coming and bowing down before him in need of help. Joseph went through years of pain and suffering. He endured years of waiting. I imagine he faced similar doubts that we all do when our plans end, and God's plan begins. I imagine him praying and asking if he understood his dreams correctly or maybe he asked God if He changed his mind. I imagine his grief as his family sold him into slavery. I imagine his anger, his confusion, his fear and his loneliness. He lost so much time with his family. How heartbreaking his season of waiting must have been. Yet, in His loving kindness, God kept His word. He used Joseph to save his own family. God used Joseph to bring his family into the promise land.

We never see the big picture. When we make our plans, no matter how great they are, we only see in part. We don't see the speed bumps, the detours or the stop signs. We never factor in seasons of waiting. If you are in the middle of planning out every day of the rest of your life, will you take some time and surrender your timetable? Will you lay it all out before the Lord and ask Him to give you His plans? If your plans have ended and God's plan has begun, can you rest in Him knowing that He is the one that sees the big picture? Just because that promise hasn't come to pass yet doesn't mean it won't. It doesn't mean you heard Him wrong. It doesn't mean your dreams are over. It simply means that God has you in the waiting. Will you dare to believe by faith that what the Lord has spoken over your life will happen? There is purpose for you right now, right where you are.

God is outside of time, but He does have your journey planned out in great detail. His heart is for you to experience joy in every moment of every day no matter what is going on around you. Our timetables keep us bound. They set us up for disappointment, bitterness, and resentment when things don't go as planned. Yet, joy is waiting for you today. There is so much freedom in surrender. When we give God our plans, He comes and gives us peace, rest and joy. He makes beauty from ashes. He restores, redeems and makes all things new. If things aren't going as you planned today, do not lose hope. Instead fix your eyes on Jesus, surrender your timetable and receive His joy. The Lord is inviting you to walk with Him through the waiting. He sees you and He has an amazing plan and purpose for your life. May you experience the fullness of His joy as you surrender your plans today.

Day Twenty-Four
Worship Is Your Weapon

*Then Abraham said to his young men, "Stay
here with the donkey; I and the boy will go over
there and worship and come again to you.
Genesis 22:5 ESV*

     The last few years we were living in the United
States before we moved to Central America, we had this
beautiful two-bedroom apartment. Of course, there was
no baby at the time, so the second bedroom was open
most of the time unless we had guests in town. It
became more of an office and study and held my piano
and guitar. It was my prayer closet, my worship space,
my writing zone and my secret place. Jesus met me
there every time I entered that sacred space. It became
very comfortable and predictable. I knew how He would
come and meet me, every time I made the space for Him
to inhabit my worship. I could sit at the piano for hours
praying and journaling. He always came. He always
comforted me. He always spoke. I always left that room
refreshed, but then the Lord asked us to follow Him
overseas. We gave away lots of stuff and had to say so
many hard "see you laters," but the hardest part for me

was walking away from that room. Of course, the Holy Spirit lives in me. Why would it be so difficult to walk away from that place? It had nothing to do with the room, but everything to do with the history and intimacy I had built with the Lord in that place. Leaving that safe place behind was my hardest goodbye.

Fast forward to our lives in the jungle and things are night and day from my prayer closet back home. In a foreign land, raising a baby who is now toddler without any family nearby has not been anywhere close too easy. I no longer had those hours of quiet singing and praying my heart out. Now, I can barely read through a chapter of the Bible in the mornings without some kind of loud interruption that leaves me returning to the same sentence time and time again. It has taken most of our time here to come up with some kind of routine where I can meet with Jesus. I had become very accustomed to my secret place routine with the quiet and the stillness. I had become so comfortable in knowing who God was in that place that it shook my world when I no longer had my quiet days. The chaos of the new left this hole as I searched for a new normal. I was still in the waiting yet struggling to find a moment of quiet with the new life we were living.

When we think of worship, we tend to think of Sunday morning. Three worship songs and a sermon. Or maybe it's blasting worship songs in the car on the way to work. Or maybe like me, it was in the stillness of the secret place that you knew worship. When we think of worship we normally think of music. One of the first passages in the Bible that mentions worship is in Genesis 22, when Abraham was getting ready to sacrifice his son, Isaac. This passage never mentions anything about music or Abraham and Isaac taking their instruments up the hill. Instead, we see a father who in obedience took the Lord at His word and moved forward by faith to sacrifice his son. It was Abraham's greatest act of worship to obediently leave the comforts of his own home and lay down the life of his only beloved son as an offering, because He loved the Lord with all of his heart, soul and strength. His trust and faith in the Lord was the greatest form of worship. It had nothing to do with music or a sermon. It was through Abraham's love of the Lord that he was able to offer one of the greatest acts of trust.

We go through many seasons on this journey with the Lord. Each season teaches us about different characteristics and attributes of who God is. We learn more and more about Him as we walk through different circumstances. He is always with us, even when we are learning a new aspect of who He is. In the silence and in the chaos, He is there. It can take time to transition between seasons as we hold tightly to the comfortable moments of what we already know. Our greatest moments of worship can come from the scary and uncomfortable seasons where we walk by faith, laying our lives down, because we love and trust the One who holds our hearts. It's the seasons of waiting where the quietness of our surroundings can teach us the sound of that still small voice once again. It's in the waiting where the different rhythms of our lives lead us to seek His face in new ways. It's in the waiting where we're able to lay aside the years of busyness and return to the joy of our salvation. The joy of knowing and loving Jesus as our first love. It's in the waiting where the Holy Spirit strips us down from the ways of the world and reminds us of who He is in every situation. Then He reminds us of who we are in Him. He reminds us,

When you pass through the waters, I will be with you; and through the rivers, they shall not overwhelm you; when you walk through fire you shall not be burned, and the flame shall not consume you. For I am the LORD your God, the Holy One of Israel, your Savior.
Isaiah 43:2-3 ESV

If you have been waiting on the Lord, the way you worship Him most likely looks different than it once did. Rest assured that this is okay. It took a long time for me to realize that worship was not just me pouring my heart out at my piano. Some days it looked like time on my knees with a puddle of tears underneath me, unable to speak or sing after my family went to sleep. Some days it looked like dancing my heart out in the few minutes of alone time until I could feel breakthrough inside of me. Some days it looked like serving my husband and daughter the best I could even when my heart was struggling to hope. Some days it was fighting to find joy when my heart was crushed by disappointment.

If you have been struggling to find your secret place where you meet with Him, where you hear His voice and where you feel His presence, just keep your eyes on Jesus. Your season may look different, but God is with you. If your prayer time is while you're washing dishes and your time in the Word looks like one sentence at a time between making breakfast and changing diapers, be encouraged that the Lord will meet you there. If you are sitting in waiting, terrified of the silence, be encouraged that the Lord will meet you there as well. In the silence and in the chaos He is there. Seasons come and go, but the Lord remains the same. Let obedience be your greatest act of worship. Let your love for Him overflow with trust, rest, peace and thanksgiving as you give Him your life as an offering. Abraham's faith blessed all the nations of the earth that day. (Genesis 22:15-18) May your time of waiting bring worship to Jesus today. He's so worthy.

Day Twenty-Five
Peace in the Silence

Peace I leave with you. My peace I give to you.
I do not give to you as the world gives.
Your heart must not be troubled or fearful.
John 14:27 HCSB

We find peace in a lot of different ways. We usually describe our lives as peaceful when everything is going exactly the way we want it to be going. We feel peace when the refrigerator is full, when the car has gas, when our kids are healthy, when the bills are paid and when our dreams are coming true. We feel peace when our prayers are answered. We feel peace when we see miracles. If you look up the definition of peace it is described as *"freedom from disturbance or tranquility."* Other words that are similar would be quiet, stillness, isolation, solitude, calmness and so on. And while having a life with no conflict or troubles is every person's dream it's not how our lives normally go.

We often times get caught up in a worldly definition of peace when we have everything exactly the way we want it. It's a false sense of peace, because everything in the world can be going well without us experiencing real tangible peace that only Jesus can give. We oftentimes base peace on the external factors of our lives when in fact, peace is an internal state of our hearts. If we truly know peace, when troubles come and we feel like our lives are falling apart, our peace is not lost. It's through the chaos that we discover the peace that only Jesus gives. This type of peace is real and lasting. This type of peace is the state of our hearts when life is crashing down around us. Sometimes I think we get peace mixed up with our other emotions. We think that in order to keep our peace we have to push every other emotion aside when trauma, stress, grief or depression hit. We tell people we have peace when in fact we're barely holding ourselves together. It is as if admitting to someone that we're sad or feeling hopeless lessens the peace we have, but that is not true peace.

When we endure through the waiting, our peace gets tested. The Lord seems to have this way of revealing to us that His peace endures the silence. His peace lasts when nothing is going right. His peace is still there when the bills aren't paid, when our kids are sick and when there's no food in the refrigerator. His peace endures through every situation because the Prince of Peace is who He is. Isaiah 9:6 says,

"For to us a child is born, to us a son is given; and the government shall be upon his shoulder, and his name shall be called Wonderful Counselor, Mighty God, Everlasting Father, Prince of Peace." ESV

Peace is Jesus. It's who He is. Peace is not a feeling that comes and goes, but a revelation of who Jesus is to us every minute of the day.

There were times in our waiting, even in the extremely hot jungle of Central America, that felt like a dark cold winter. Through every step of our process in bringing our daughter home I would tell the world that I had peace even though my heart felt like it had been shattered into a million pieces. For so long I had formed my identity in the belief that, if the Lord was answering my prayers and if things were going my way, I was loved. My peace was based on the status of my world. If I felt content, I had peace. If I felt loved, I had peace. The silence in those winter seasons of waiting reveals the lies we believe about who God is and who we are. It also shows us where our thinking aligns more with the world than the Word. It makes me think about the story in Mark 4:35-41 when Jesus calms the storm. Jesus and the disciples were on a boat when a great windstorm arose. The boat was filling with water and the disciples were afraid. Jesus was asleep and the panicked men woke him up. They were with the Prince of Peace and were still full of fear! Jesus then told the sea, *"Peace! Be still!"* and the wind ceased, and the sea was calm. The first question Jesus asked the disciples after he calmed the storm was, *"Why are you so afraid? Have you still no faith?"*

When troubles arrive in my life, I often think about how Jesus is not moved by my fear. He's not anxiously waiting to see how the issues in my life are going to work out. He's in every moment of my day. He knows the storms I face and in His loving kindness He speaks, "*Peace! Be still!*". The silence of waiting often leaves our restless hearts anxious. It's in the silence where the Holy Spirit lovingly speaks truth to the areas of our life that need convicting. So often I think if we truly knew how loved we are we would never live another day without peace. We can feel peace, yet true peace is always present in our lives through Jesus. That means that when our lives are falling apart, we can live victoriously because we know that Jesus is with us. Peace is not just the absence of troubles. Living in peace is living free, whole and complete because of who Jesus is. Jesus says in John 16:33,

"I have told you these things so that in Me you may have peace. In this world you will have trouble, but take heart! I have overcome the world." NIV

You can walk through hard times and still have peace. You can experience fear, trauma, stress and anxiety and still have peace. Why? Because living in peace is making a conscious choice to allow Jesus to speak to your emotions, to your storms and to your heart. As you wait on the Lord and the silence draws out the lies you've believed you can choose to surrender those feelings to the Lord and by faith, receive the peace that Jesus died to give you. Your heart can be at rest through all things because you know you are loved by the Prince of Peace. You will be okay today because Jesus is with you. You have peace today because Jesus is with you. Spend some time reading Mark 4:35-41. Ask the Lord to show you the areas of your heart that are experiencing a false peace. Then ask Him to replace that peace with *His* peace. When you encounter real, everlasting peace you will feel like you're breathing for the very first time. Praise Jesus for who He is and how He is revealing Himself to you through this time. He is building a foundation in you that can never be shaken. May you live in peace as you continue walking through your waiting.

Day Twenty-Six
Joy Unspeakable

And now my head shall be lifted up above my enemies all around me; Therefore I will offer sacrifices of joy in His tabernacle; I will sing, yes, I will sing praises to the LORD.
Psalms 27:6 NKJV

I usually do a lot of fasting in the spring between Passover and Pentecost. One year during my waiting, as I sat with Jesus asking Him what I needed to fast from, this specific time His words caught me off guard. It wasn't a social media fast, saying goodbye to sugar, or eating nothing but vegetables. This time the Holy Spirit specifically asked me to give Him my joy. My first thought was that I had no idea what that even means. Father, you are my joy. How do I give it back to you? How do I sacrifice joy to you? It was clear He wasn't asking me to give Him all my joy in a way that was going to leave the next several weeks miserable. But instead, it was an invitation to step *into* His joy, to experience His fullness of joy through all circumstances. Well, that didn't seem like a fast to me. Yet, as I sat with Him and unpacked what it meant I realized that through the years I had come to expect disappointments. I was looking for them. What bad or disappointing thing was going to happen next? What did I need to prepare for so that my spirit wasn't crushed? What kind of walls could I put around my heart to protect myself from what's next? At some point through my years of waiting and most likely even before the waiting began, I'd laid down my joy. I forgot what it meant to enjoy life. I had become so focused on just surviving each day that I forgot to stop, breathe and rejoice.

It's hard to enjoy the life we've been given when we're waiting for the next defeat. It's hard to consider it all joy when we're constantly bombarded by circumstances that just aren't going our way. Sometimes we even struggle to receive joy. Is it okay for us to feel joy when life looks like it's crashing down around us? God has given us so many different emotions. We feel grief and anger. We feel compassion and love, yet when it comes to joy, not only do we sometimes struggle to receive it, but we also occasionally feel bad for even feeling it. In a world that is full of death and grief, how can we possibly feel and live a joyful life? Yet, joy is Jesus. It's the way of the Kingdom. Joy leads to the breakthroughs. Joy is our inheritance. Jesus died so that we would have life and life abundantly. He died so that we could have joy unspeakable and full of glory no matter what is going on around us. As the Holy Spirit often does, during my fast He convicted me that I hadn't been giving Him joy. I hadn't been enjoying the life He blessed me with. I suddenly realized that our days are numbered. I realized how many days I'd already wasted being miserable. I realized how many days I spent discontent because I was still waiting for the Lord to answer my prayers. I have so much joy available to me every single day. I have a beautiful family that God has given me to enjoy. I have food in the refrigerator to make delicious healthy meals for my family every day to keep them healthy. I have a comfortable bed. I have money in the bank. I have a cell phone that can connect me to people all over the world in seconds. I could go on and on. We have the choice every day to choose joy or to live bound by disappointment. I don't know how many days on earth I have. I also don't know how many days my family and friends have, but I do know that I will rejoice in every day that I get to love them and serve them. Every day is a blessing. On our worst days, we still have so many things to be thankful for. We still have so many reasons to choose joy. Philippians 4:8 says,

"Finally brothers, whatever is true, whatever is honorable, whatever is just, whatever is pure, whatever is lovely, whatever is commendable - if there is any moral excellence and if there is any praise - dwell on these things." HCSB

If there is anything worthy of praise dwell on these things! You may not have picked the season you're in. You may be struggling to figure out your next steps. You may have already run out of next steps, and you literally can do nothing but wait on the Lord. If your heart is surrendered to the Lord, then you can experience fullness of joy. Right here. Right now. Right where you are. The Lord has you where you are for a purpose, and He did not call you to this point to be miserable. He's inviting you to receive His joy while you wait. When I ask my daughter to wait to eat her favorite cookie until after she eats her healthy lunch, I'm not asking her to be miserable. I simply want what's best for her. I want her little body to be full of life. Of course, at three years old she doesn't understand this, so she cries and gets angry thinking that I'm just trying to keep dessert from her. I've intentionally prepared her lunch with love knowing exactly what she needs to live abundantly. I know that if she fills up on the good things that fuel her body, the cookie will taste even sweeter. Choose joy unspeakable today. Choose to celebrate. Choose to enjoy the table that the Lord has prepared for you.

It had been in the upper 90s one week while the construction guys we had hired had been outside working on the Rescue Center we are building. They worked outside more than eight hours a day. It was hot and miserable, yet as they worked and listened to a soccer game, I could hear them across the yard screaming and cheering for joy when their team made a goal. Their joy over that one goal made me want to run outside and see what was going on. What if we lived our lives in such a way that made people want to run and see what we were so joyful about every single day? What if we enjoyed this beautiful life we've been given? What if we gave Jesus our joy as an offering? What would it look like? It's a lot harder than I ever thought it would be. It's possible to feel grief and still experience joy. It's possible to be angry about something, but still walk in joy. When we examine our emotions through the cross, it's impossible not to experience fullness of joy. When I'm tempted by anxious thoughts, anger or grief I now remind myself that I'm giving Jesus joy as an offering today. When I receive the gifts, He's given I'm overwhelmed with thankfulness, and I rest in who He is. The emotions fade even when the circumstances don't change and joy overflows because God has been so good, so kind and so very faithful. What is keeping you from joy unspeakable today? If you've been struggling to feel joy lately, I pray that you would experience the love and joy of Jesus right where you are. I pray that you would live in such a way that the people around you would be drawn to the sound of your joy. Enjoy your life today and every day no matter what is happening. Today is a gift and there will never be another day like it.

Sometimes seasons of waiting can feel like the end. It can be hard to see what's next. But it's not the end. The Lord is maturing you so that you can fully and freely possess your promise land. When you choose to walk in joy on this journey it doesn't matter what tomorrow holds, because we know the One who holds it. Allow yourself to receive the joy that God has so freely given. Allow Him to heal your heart from the things that are keeping you from delighting in Him. Jesus is so worthy of our joy!

This is the day the LORD has made; let us rejoice and be glad in it. Psalm 118:24 HCSB

Day Twenty-Seven
Resting for The First Time

Come to me, all who labor and are heavy laden,
and I will give you rest. Take my yoke upon you,
and learn from me, for I am gentle and lowly in
heart, and you will find rest for your souls. For
my yoke is easy, and my burden is light.
Matthew 11:28-30 ESV

Rest has always felt like a foreign word to me. What is it? How do I do it? Is it really necessary? When I picture the word rest, I see myself on vacation sitting on a white, sandy beach staring off into the crystal-clear ocean. That looks like rest to me. But how often do we all truly get to escape our daily lives into that perfect dream vacation. In fact, every time I have been blessed to experience that dream rest, I usually need a vacation from the vacation when we return to reality. Have you ever experienced exhaustion from rest? Have you ever needed a vacation from your vacation?

There are so many definitions of rest, in fact, you probably have a different definition than I do. There is physical rest, mental rest, emotional rest, spiritual rest, vacation rest, Sabbath rest and on and on the list goes. I thought resting would get easier the longer we waited. As the seasons of waiting changed and parts of life got easier and my heart was healing, I thought I could finally rest. But it was only when I actually started trying to rest that I realized how much of my life was spent just trying to stay busy. For years I described my life as 'busy'. When someone asked how I was, I would always respond with, "I'm good, just busy." It was as if part of my identity was classified under the word 'busy'. I had this constant need to fill my days with stuff. It wasn't bad stuff, but it wasn't stuff the Lord was asking me to do either. We do a lot of good things in life that aren't necessarily God things. The busy in my life was fueled by this desire I had to earn God's love and please people. It was as if, somewhere deep inside my heart, I thought I could earn more of God's love. Of course, we know that it is by grace we have been saved, a gift from God, not by our own doing. (Ephesians 2:8-9) And of course we know we're not supposed to focus on pleasing people. (Galatians 1:10) Yet there I was, trying to fill every moment of my day, every night of the week, every calendar space, with stuff. Then the Lord took us to the jungle of Central America where there really wasn't much stuff. The Lord quickly dealt with my heart about busyness. He stripped it all away. There I sat, just me and Jesus, my heart racing, because all the things inside that I was trying to avoid could no longer be covered by busy. All the emotions of unanswered prayers and impossible situations on top of years of burn out left me feeling like the weight of the world was on my shoulders.

When I say there wasn't much stuff to do in the jungle of Central America it wasn't as if there was nothing to do. Learning to live in a completely different culture left me drained and exhausted as I learned to do the simplest tasks all over again. I no longer had the luxuries of home. Dishes were washed by hand in a *pila*, a sink that held the day's water supply. The cement floor was mopped by a broom with a piece of cloth over the top. Electricity would come and go throughout the day. It wasn't as if one thing was too different or too hard to deal with, but it was all the little things piled together that left me barely breathing. Our banking was different. Our grocery shopping was different. Our driving was different. The modern-day conveniences were different. We were raising our baby in a land we really truly knew nothing about. I often felt like I had done more before nine o'clock in the morning than I ever did in one day back home. Living was just different. We tried for the first couple years to become like the natives. We said yes to everything. We pushed ourselves to our breaking point.

Then, one day we realized we were done. We were way past burnt out. We couldn't be the people that we were trying so hard to be. There was no amount of sleep that would have restored our weary souls. It was as if the Lord opened up this season of rest for us. There was no specific moment in time that I remember having this switch take place. It was as subtle as the seasons changing. One day we were killing ourselves in busyness and the next we were free to say no to all the things that kept us bound in busyness. It was as if the Lord, in His loving kindness, invited us to walk with Him in freedom to be who He created us to be. It was no longer about trying to be like the people we were sent to serve. Instead, it was this deep calling from the Holy Spirit to truly *"come all you who are weary and heavy laden"*. It was the Lord calling us to himself. It was through this call to come and rest that I believe our family experienced the greatest revelation of our true identity of who we are as sons and daughters. Through this revelation, it was as if we were free to just say no. No to all the stuff we felt obligated to do, all the things that kept us from rest. When we stopped being busy, just for the sake of being busy and actually started praying about what we were supposed to do and when we were supposed to do it, we were free to experience real rest.

Our days were no longer defined by rest days and busy days. Instead, we were doing what the Lord had asked of us and nothing more. We were free to seek Him, to come to Him. And it's in Him that we're able to experience rest no matter what we're doing. Rest is no longer something we schedule on the calendar. Rest is a lifestyle. It's how we operate. It was such a battle to enter into this lifestyle of rest. When we started saying no to things, we looked weird to everyone. We were misunderstood. We were gossiped about. People thought something was wrong with us, but we fought through our issues with pleasing people. We fought through our internal struggles of saying no to things we felt obligated to do. It can still be a battle, even to this day, but through this journey of entering rest we have experienced freedom. We have experienced rest for the first time. It's not a vacation type rest. It's a daily rest that lets our hearts cry *'it is well with my soul'*. It *is* well with my soul now, even though my prayers haven't been answered the way I want. It is well with my soul when I don't know how I'm going to pay my bills. It is well with my soul when the world looks like it is crashing down around me. It is well with my soul, because I have found rest in Christ alone. The world gives us every reason to fear and worry, but Jesus gives us rest. Jesus gives us peace. Jesus gives us joy. All we have to do is come to Him. It's one of His promises to us.

"Come to me, all who labor and are heavy laden, and I will give you rest." Matthew 11:28 ESV

Have you experienced true rest? Not the kind of rest that helps you escape from your daily life, but the kind of rest that gives you freedom to experience abundant life. If you haven't felt rest for your soul in a long time, start by asking the Lord what you need to say no to. Create space in your day, month, season and year to do nothing more than be with Jesus. Let go of the things that keep you busy and the things that leave you distracted. You can be doing a lot of great things, but they aren't necessarily what the Lord is asking you to be doing right now. Start by asking God what you need to let go of. Remember it's okay to be misunderstood by the world around you. The Lord is introducing you to a new way to live. He's pulling you close to His heart so that you know who He is and who you are in Him. Resting is such a crucial part of this waiting journey. Will you allow the Lord to walk you into freedom? Receive His rest today. Your life will never be the same.

Day Twenty-Eight
Sabbath Rest

Therefore, a Sabbath rest remains for God's people.
For the person who has entered His rest has rested
from his own works, just as God did from His. Let us
then make effort to enter that rest, so that no one
will fall into the same pattern of disobedience.
Hebrews 4:9-11 HCSB

One of the best things our family has ever done is practice the discipline of a Sabbath rest. A day set aside from the rest of the week to proclaim as holy. The word holy can also be described as set apart, sacred, or dedicated. While labeling a day with the word holy seems religious, it is actually one of the most amazing gifts we can receive as God's children. While it was a law for the Hebrews in the Old Testament it has been given to us as a gift through Jesus. A gift to receive with freedom and joy. It was probably a year into our waiting and after multiple years of being exhausted that we started setting aside one day a week to do no work. A day to simply be together as a family. A day to set aside and honor as holy. A day to worship, rest, and have some fun. A day to recharge from the usual busy week. It's interesting that the concept of practicing the

Sabbath, which is talked about in both the Old and New Testament is very rarely practiced in our Christian homes. Yes, most of us go to church on Sundays, but the Sabbath is so much more than that. It's so much more than meeting with a community of like-minded believers. The Sabbath is a gift for us. It's a gift that most of us have overlooked or pushed aside. It's like a teenager receiving a Christmas gift of fine china from their grandparents. We've all been given a gift we are excited to open yet met with disappointment when it's not what we thought it was going to be. It could be a gift that was passed down from generation to generation. A gift with history and great value. So, what does the teenager do with fine china? They pack it away to collect dust. They've received the gift, but it won't be until years later when they have a family of their own that they discover how they had received such a grand and beautiful treasure.

It's the same with the Sabbath. From the beginning in Genesis 2:3 we're told,

"So God blessed the seventh day and made it holy, because on it God rested from all his work that he had done in creation." ESV

And then again in Exodus 20:8-11.

"Remember the Sabbath day, to keep it holy." ESV

It's a gift we've been given from the beginning, yet most of us push it aside, thinking that it's not a gift for us today. We automatically think it doesn't apply to us because it's part of the Old Testament. We think it's a law and then justify within our hearts that we don't need it. Could it be that the Sabbath is one of God's greatest blessings for us, His kids? For some reason so many of us are stuck in this mindset that we constantly have to be doing great things for God. We try to do so many great things for Him that we leave ourselves tired, burnt out, and full of worldly thoughts and desires. We somehow forget that God has never asked us to do great things for Him, but great things *with* Him. We get so caught up in our own way of doing great things that we forget to stop and rest. We forget that our highest calling is ministering to His heart. It's in the moments of rest where our hearts can truly untangle from the world and worship Jesus. It's in the Sabbath where we build intimacy with the Father. When we stop from our work and the busyness of our week to minister to His heart our lives remain full. It's through the Sabbath where we're able to be filled to overflowing. It's where we are centered and refocused so that we do not spend the rest of our week in survival mode. We weren't created to live in chronic stress, just barely surviving. We were meant to live an abundant life. We were meant to thrive.

When my family started practicing the Sabbath, I will be honest, it was extremely uncomfortable. It took quite a while for us to figure out what Sabbath looked like for us individually and also as a family. We were finally starting to live from a place of rest, but taking a day off still seemed odd. Our ministry in the jungle involves a lot of people in need coming to our house every day all day. How do we just turn it off? How do we stop serving the people around us so that we can minister to God's heart? It took a huge transition in our mindset. Turning away someone in need or waiting a day to address a situation felt like it went totally against what we believed. Yet, we knew God loved those people more than we could. We knew that He was their Provider. We knew that God was calling us to practice the Sabbath, so we fought to enter His rest. And miraculously when we stepped out in faith and surrendered our restlessness to Jesus, He turned our striving into thriving and our burnout into joy.

I remember one Sabbath I woke up with the sink full of dishes and a huge pile of laundry that needed to be folded. The house was a mess and meals needed to be prepared. But, instead of jumping into the day, I went outside and sat. I sat and watched my daughter play. I let my body and mind rest as I watched her play. I stopped hustling just to be. Everything still got done that day. The dishes got washed. The laundry was folded. The family was fed. Not everything on my long list of things to do got done, but I was more productive that week after practicing rest than I was on any week that I spent striving.

Our Sabbath looks different every week. Sometimes we wash each other's feet and take communion together. Sometimes we play together. Sometimes we all take naps. Sometimes we listen to a sermon together as a family. Other times we spend individual time with Jesus. Some weeks our Sabbath is on a Saturday and other weeks it's on a Sunday. Some weeks it's even during the week. Regardless of when it is or what it looks like, we set a day aside each week to rest. We set a day aside to honor the Lord and to praise Him for the end of one week and the beginning of a new one. No matter how difficult or how great the week has been we know that in order for us to thrive, we each need the Sabbath, both individually and as a family. We left the gift of the Sabbath unopened for far too long.

God made the Sabbath for us. Will you enter His rest? The waiting does something inside of us. It realigns the areas of our lives that are not aligned with God's heart. If you have been struggling to enter into God's rest, will you try making the Sabbath a part of your week? One of God's great gifts is waiting for you to open it up. Dig into the Bible today and discover what God says about the Sabbath, then make a plan to enjoy a Sabbath each week. What does it look like for you and your family? How can you set a day aside to honor the Lord? As you sit at the feet of Jesus today, ask Him to help you enjoy the Sabbath. Then watch as burnout turns to joy and peace in His presence.

Day Twenty-Nine
Living Out of Overflow

The LORD is my shepherd; there is nothing I lack. He lets me lie down in green pastures; He leads me beside quiet waters. He renews my life; He leads me along the right paths for His name's sake. Even when I go through the darkest valley, I fear no danger, for You are with me; Your rod and Your staff - they comfort me. You prepare a table before me in the presence of my enemies; You anoint my head with oil; my cup overflows. Only goodness and faithful love will pursue me all the days of my life, and I will dwell in the house of the LORD as long as I live.
Psalms 23 HCSB

So much of the waiting can feel like you're walking through the wilderness all alone. It can feel like a fight. Some days it can feel like you're doing everything you can just to survive. As days go on and seasons change you begin to change too. Your situation may look exactly the same. You may not have seen any answered prayers or felt any breakthrough, but as you walk through the process of waiting with the Lord, I can guarantee that things inside you have been shifting. As the Lord has been healing you and realigning you through this journey. I can imagine your outlook on life looks different. I bet you feel lighter and feel like you truly can breathe for the first time in a long time. Yes, there may be some rough days, but perhaps you've gotten used to this waiting season. Some things may even feel a little comfortable now. There's a new pattern and rhythm to your days. And yet, the waiting continues.

For so long I felt like my waiting was about me. Maybe I just wasn't getting what the Lord was trying to teach me. Maybe I haven't grown enough. Maybe my faith isn't where it needs to be. I was still looking for things to do to get us out of our circumstances. After walking through the many seasons of waiting, I now think differently. I act differently. I respond differently. I am a completely different person now than when the Lord first invited me to wait on Him. Nothing in my physical circumstances of waiting has changed. You know, the funny thing is, even though the Lord hasn't answered my prayers the way I thought He would or the way I wanted Him to, I can tell you that I love Jesus more today than I did on my first day of waiting. I love Him more now than I did then.

He is my everything. I know Him better today than I did on day one, because He proved Himself true and faithful when I was barely hanging on. It's through this hard and crushing season of waiting that the Lord so kindly removed pieces of me that were not of Him so that He could heal and restore those areas of my life with His resurrection life. My waiting has been the 23rd Psalm. Verse one says,

"The LORD is my shepherd. I shall not lack." HCSB

For so long I felt like I was lacking. I didn't have what I thought I needed. But as I look back over this season of waiting, I don't see any lack at all. I see my shepherd who protected me and guided me ever so gently through my pain and questions. I have no lack. I have no wants. All I want is more of Him. In Him I have everything I need. So subtly He makes these changes in our lives and we normally don't even see Him working. If you would have asked me a while ago if I believed I lacked things or was in want, my answer would have been a resounding yes. Even so, I can now stand here and tell you I never lacked. He was faithful through it all.

He makes me lie down in green pastures.
He leads me beside still waters. He restores my soul.
He leads me in paths of righteousness for his name's sake.
Psalm 23:2-3 HCSB

So much of our time waiting on the Lord has been in isolation. It has felt at times like the Lord picked us up and dropped us off on a deserted island. At first it felt like torture. It felt as if we were being punished for something. When I look back over all these days in the wilderness, I now can see that the isolation was one of the greatest waiting gifts. He made me lie down in green pastures and led me beside still waters. He gave me a place to unravel far away from the world. He gave me a place of safety and peace where I could heal and be restored. He used the quietness of our days to lead me in righteousness for His glory. The isolation wasn't a punishment. It was a gift of time and space that allowed me to rest and breathe while I was figuring out how to live again.

Even though I walk through the shadow of death
I will fear no evil, for you are with me;
your rod and your staff they comfort me.
Psalm 23:4 HCSB

At times during our waiting, it felt like the world was ending. It felt like there was no hope. It felt like there was no light at the end of the tunnel. As I chose to worship, I was met by the comforter every step of the way. He surrounded us with the people and things we needed to move forward in our process every day. The Lord would open doors and close doors. He would teach us to follow the small whisper of His voice so that we were ever so close to Him. He would hide us in the shadow of His wing. Because we know Him as Comforter, we have nothing to fear.

He prepares a table before me
in the presence of my enemies. He anoints
my head with oil and my cup overflows!
Psalm 23:5 HCSB

We have victory. We may still be waiting, but I feel victory inside me now more than ever. We have victory, because Jesus is victorious. My cup is overflowing with Him. Every battle that He has walked me through has resulted in more of Him and less of me. My cup is overflowing with love, peace, joy, rest, trust, faith, righteousness, and so on. God does not leave us empty. He redeems and He restores! He wants our lives to overflow with His goodness and mercy. He wants our lives to overflow with His love. It's through the waiting where He cleans out the junk in our hearts so that He can fill us with every good thing.

> *Surely goodness and mercy shall follow me*
> *all the days of our lives so that we can*
> *dwell in the house of the LORD forever!*
> *Psalm 23:6 HCSB*

Surely goodness and mercy! The more Jesus we have the more we look like light to the world. The more of Jesus we have, the better we are at serving our spouse and children. The more of Jesus we have, the more we're able to serve our communities. The more of Jesus we have, the more we want Him. The more of Jesus we have, the more we can live from a place of overflow.

Things overflow from our hearts every day. What we fill our lives with determines what flows out. Has the Lord been healing and restoring places of your heart while you wait? If so, He's been creating space in your cup to fill you with more of Jesus. He wants Jesus to flow out of you. He is never going to leave you dry. He has victory sealed over your situation. Will you trust Him to be your shepherd? Will you allow Him to fill you with every good thing He has for you?

I pray that your cup overflows today. I pray that you can look back and see how faithful and good God has been to you even while you wait on Him. There is purpose in your waiting. You can live out that purpose today. You don't have to wait until your prayers are answered. As you wait, be filled with every good thing so that the Lord can be glorified in your waiting. When God says wait, He's not just filling you up He's preparing you to overflow.

Day Thirty
Hard Reset

And I will lay sinews upon you, and will cause
flesh to come upon you, and cover you with skin,
and put breath in you, and you shall live, and
you shall know that I am the LORD.
Ezekiel 37:6 ESV

I struggled so much with being misunderstood while we waited. We were in a culture where we didn't speak the same language. It didn't matter that I took three years of Spanish in High School. It didn't matter that I practiced every day. It didn't matter that I wanted so badly to communicate. It didn't matter that I lived in the country for three years. There was still a language barrier. Yes, it did get easier. Yes, my head didn't hurt after every conversation like it did in the beginning, but three years into the wait and my heart still longed to be understood. Our process in bringing our daughter home did not go according to how we prayed or how we thought it would go. It turned into a long and complicated battle. Year after year would pass without any type of hope or movement. It was partly because of red tape and politics, but also because of a culture that just operates slowly. People back home didn't understand. It was as frustrating for them as it was for us. That frustration led to lots of advice and lots of new connections that led nowhere. We knew we needed a miracle from the beginning. It was no surprise to us. The surprise came after a season of miracles when we stepped out in faith and the Lord didn't give us the miracle when we thought He was going to.

We were misunderstood. Misunderstood daily by the culture we were living in and by friends and family that didn't understand why we weren't coming home. *We* didn't even understand why we weren't coming home, but there we were, waiting. Waiting for our miracle. As the Lord was working inside of us and we were being led by the Holy Spirit to do certain things and not do other things along the way, we were even more misunderstood. People couldn't see the work that was being done on the inside of us. They didn't understand why we stopped doing things we used to do or why we had new boundaries set in place. They didn't understand the journey the Lord had us on or the process that it took to get there. How could they have understood? The changes in our lives were internal ones. Everything on the outside looked exactly the same. All they saw was a dead end to our long painful waiting.

I'm guessing you have felt misunderstood at some point along the way too. When God does a work inside of us, it doesn't always change our circumstances.

Sometimes He asks us to remove things from our lives or asks us to establish certain boundaries so that He can do all that He wants to do inside of us. It's better to say no to people and face being misunderstood than to walk somewhere He's not asking us to go. Other people cannot possibly understand the journey of waiting you're on. That's okay. The Lord has them on their own journey. While you feel misunderstood today it does not mean that you will feel misunderstood forever. Part of the journey is learning to walk with the Holy Spirit, no matter what the cost. Learning to walk close to the Father's heart when everything inside you is trying to run to where you're comfortable is such a big part of this process. Will you dare to be misunderstood for the glory of the Lord?

I think about The Valley of Dry Bones in Ezekiel 37:1-14. In a vision from the LORD, Ezekiel was told to prophesy over some bones. If I were Ezekiel, I probably would have thought that I misunderstood. "Lord, you want me to tell these bones to live? They are just bones. They don't look like much." The situation was dead. Yet, as Ezekiel obeyed and prophesied over the bones, there was a rattling sound, and the bones came together. As the bones came together, flesh grew on them, but there was no breath in them. Ezekiel was then told again to prophesy so that breath would come upon them, and it did. The bones were now alive and stood on their feet as an exceedingly great army. Do not let your dead situations, your unanswered prayers or your delayed miracles keep you from the promises the Lord has spoken over your life. Your life may be misunderstood by those around you. Your life may not even make sense to *you* right now, but God is breathing on your life. He has placed His Spirit within you so that you can live!

At this point in your waiting, you are only still actually waiting if the Lord truly told you to wait on Him. You are only holding on to hope if you know, deep down inside, that this is God's will for your life. So do not stop prophesying what He's spoken over your situation. Your life may just look like a pile of dead bones to the rest of the world, but God is breathing on you! This is your hard reset. It's like when your computer or phone just freezes up and the only thing that will fix it is a hard reset. A hard reset on a device restores it to factory settings. It erases all the applications that the user installed. This is your moment of hard reset. This is when God has brought you to a point in your waiting to restore all things inside of you. It doesn't matter if you're misunderstood, talked about or persecuted. All the world sees are the dead bones, but you know that God is doing miracles in your heart. You know that God is restoring all things in your life, so prophesy to your situation. Prophesy that God would breathe on your problem and watch as everything changes.

You are about to live the abundant life that Jesus died and rose again for you to have. Will you allow the Lord to breathe on you? Will you partner with Him and hold tight to His promises? Will you dig deep into His Word and seek Him, above all else? God will perform the impossible in your life. When God's Spirit is present, we are enabled to live. The Lord is placing a hard reset on your life. Through this process of waiting, parts of you have died, parts have been pruned and parts have looked absolutely hopeless, but God is restoring every part of you to the way He originally created you to be and to live. The factory settings. He is making all things new! Spend some time reading Ezekiel 37:1-14 today. As you spend time at the feet of Jesus, prophecy God's Word over your life. Prophesy to the dead bones in your situation and watch as God breathes His Spirit and does the impossible, once again.

But those who trust in the LORD will renew their strength; they will soar on wings like eagles; they will run and not grow weary; they will walk and not faint.
Isaiah 40:31 HCSB

Day Thirty-One
Bearing Fruit

I have spoken these things to you so that
My joy may be in you and your joy may be complete.
John 15:11 HCSB

There is this tree in the backyard of our home in Central America. It carries a fruit called a paterna which is a long green bean like pod that holds large seeds with fruit inside. For many years our paterna trees here have produced an abundance of fruit. We would give away maybe hundreds or thousands every year. The kids in our neighborhood just love them. But, one year some type of vine came on one of our paterna trees and wrapped itself around tight. So tight that it started to kill the tree. It barely produced any fruit that year. The tree looked dead on the outside. It barely had any leaves and as most dead trees do, it just looked sad. We cut the vine off and waited to see if it would come back to life and after a few months there was still no change. We then debated if we needed to cut the whole tree down.

We really liked this tree and also having so much fruit to give away every year, so instead we decided to prune it. When I say prune it, I mean that we actually cut about half of it away. It looked quite ridiculous as a very tall, bare tree. As weeks went by, we forgot about the tree, because it was basically dead. If we had a chainsaw, it probably would have been cut down. But then, out of nowhere, it suddenly started growing branches and these beautiful green leaves. The tree that we thought was dead was surely alive and well.

How many times in our lives do we get bound up by a vine? Sin can so easily entangle us. Sometimes pruning our heart looks just like removing the sin and untangling the vine. In other situations, the Lord in His loving kindness has to cut off parts of us. Mindsets that aren't aligned with Him. Behavior that keeps us from walking in righteousness. Pain and hurt that has us bound. The pruning of the Lord can feel quite painful at times. It can feel and sometimes even look like the Paterna tree in our yard. It can feel and look like part of us or part of our lives have been cut off. It can feel and look like we're dead on the inside, maybe even on the outside too.

This is what our time in the wilderness looked like. For most of our time in the waiting, it looked like things were dead. There was no movement on our miracle and at times it felt like the Lord had chopped off parts of our lives and parts of ourselves as He walked us through this process of waiting. As we endured each season that came, we realized the Lord was doing the exact same thing to our hearts. He was unraveling the vines that were killing us spiritually, emotionally, mentally and even physically. He was teaching us to abide in Him. Our hearts desire somewhere along the way turned from wanting our own way to wanting His. We walked through the surrendering, the desire to understand, the confusion, the disappointment and the crushing and we met Jesus every step of the way. He proved Himself faithful and true. He walked with us through our wandering and questions. He comforted us when we were lonely and simply trying to survive. He pruned us so that we could bear more fruit for His glory. He returned us to our first love, Jesus. From there our waiting changed.

I am the true vine, and my Father is the vine dresser. Every branch in me that does not bear fruit he takes away, and every branch that does bear fruit he prunes, that it may bear more fruit. Already you are clean because of the word that I have spoken to you. Abide in me, and I in you. As the branch cannot bear fruit by itself, unless it abides in the vine, neither can you, unless you abide in me. I am the vine, you are the branches. Whoever abides in me and I in him, he it is that bears much fruit, for apart from me you can do nothing. If anyone does not abide in me he is thrown away like a branch and withers; and the branches are gathered, thrown into the fire, and burned. If you abide in me and my words abide in you,

*ask whatever you wish, and it will be done for you. By this
my Father is glorified, that you bear much fruit and so
prove to be my disciples. As the Father has loved me,
so have I loved you. Abide in my love. If you keep my
commandments, you will abide in my love, just as I have
kept my Father's commandments and abide in his love.
These things I have spoken to you, that my joy may
be in you, and that your joy may be full.*
John 15:1-11 ESV

It was the pruning that led us to joy! It led us to
freedom! When the Lord prunes us, it's only so that we
can bear more fruit. It's only so that He may be glorified.
It's only so that we can live in true freedom as we
become everything God created us to be. There is joy in
the waiting. There is freedom there too. If the Lord has
been pruning you, be encouraged because the new
beautiful green branches are about to appear. What
looks dead will come alive again. You will bear more
fruit. The key is to abide in Him. Walk with the Lord
through the process. Abide in Him. Let Him abide in you.
The pruning in your life is not to harm you, but to give
you fullness of joy. You will live again! As you wait on
the Lord, I pray that you would be filled and
overflowing with resurrection life. May you walk with
Jesus through every season knowing that as you abide
in Him your life is bringing glory to the Father. May
your cup overflow with joy today as you rest and abide
in Jesus!

Day Thirty-Two
Harvest Season

Don't be deceived: God is not mocked. For whatever a man sows he will also reap, because the one who sows to his flesh will reap corruption from the flesh, but the one who sows to the Spirit will reap eternal life from the Spirit. So we must not get tired of doing good, for we will reap at the proper time if we don't give up.
Galatians 6:7-9 HCSB

One of the most beautiful things about the jungle is that everything is green and growing. One part of our time in Central America as missionaries involved building a place to care for orphans and widows along with a place for mission teams to come and stay to serve our region. The building process was incredibly slow and frustrating. Every day the prices were higher, and more material was needed. It took a long time to learn that God was moving at His own speed through this process too. As our hearts were changing through our waiting and our desire became only Jesus, we experienced a newfound joy. We started enjoying things once again. We started seeing all the blessings instead of all the disappointments of not getting our way. We were in harvest season. All the seeds that we had sown through the process of waiting were starting to sprout up. We were seeing the fruit of the midnight hours of worship. We could see how the painful process of learning to endure and persevere was leading us out into joy and freedom. We could finally feel peace and rest after choosing faith and trust day after day through seasons of fear and worry.

One of the things I loved as we prepared the land was planting fruit trees. It brought me so much joy. Whether they were seeds planted or small plants that we transplanted I could see the vision the Lord had given us to serve orphans and widows. As we watched them grow day after day and year after year, we began to see the fruit of our labor. Some trees, like the papaya, grew really fast. We had fruit within the first year. Every day it was taller providing shade and food for our home. Another tree was the banana that sprouted a giant new leaf every couple days. Then others like the coconut tree and the orange tree grew much much slower. They were alive and well, but we knew the fruit they would bring wouldn't be ready for us to enjoy during our time there. Instead, they were planted with future generations in mind. So that those we would one day serve would be able to enjoy the shade and eat of the fruit long after we were gone.

The same is true of your waiting. From day one, the Lord has been preparing you for your harvest season. You have most likely been sowing and sowing without seeing much fruit. Some fruit may sprout up quickly and other things that you have sown may seem dormant. There will come a swift change of seasons when you will begin to see what the Lord has been doing in your life through all the days you waited on Him. You will see that every seed you have sown was not forgotten. You will see that every step of faith and every moment you chose to trust instead of fear will leave you with abundance. An abundance of fruit that brings glory to Jesus. More importantly, you will have walked with God through the process of waiting, leaving you full of Him. You will know Him deeper and more intimately. You will feel full after a season of waiting that often feels more like lack than overflow.

The Lord is preparing to send you out. This whole journey of waiting has been preparing you to boldly go forth and proclaim His name to the nations. He's been molding you and forming you. He's been teaching you about His heart and how to walk in righteousness. He's done things in your wilderness that could not be done in front of the world. Though the journey might not be over yet, He will finish what He started. The seeds that you have sown when no one was looking will bear great fruit, not only in your life, but in the generations to come. The Lord has so often reminded me throughout the waiting that my waiting is not just about me. It's not just about my family or those that see our lives. Our waiting is about what the Lord is doing in His Church among the nations. How gracious He is that He would choose to use us for His glory so that His name would be magnified throughout the earth.

The Lord is preparing His bride, the Church. He's preparing us so that what is placed in our hearts bears fruit and yields a beautiful harvest.

The Lord desires for us to know Him. He desires us to love Him. He wants the seeds planted in our lives to grow deep roots so that we are not shaken when trials come. Matthew 13 explains the parable of the sower.

Hear then the parable of the sower: When anyone hears the word of the kingdom and does not understand it, the evil one comes and snatches away what has been sow in his heart. This is what was sown along the path. As for what was sown on rocky ground, this one who hears the word and immediately receives it with joy, yet he has no root in himself, but endures for a while, and when tribulation or persecution arises on account of the word, immediately he falls away. As for what was sown among thorns, this is the one who hears the word, but the cares of the world and the deceitfulness of riches choke the word, and it proves unfruitful. As for what was sown on good soil, this is the one who hears the word and understands it. He indeed bears fruit and yields, in one case a hundredfold, in another sixty, and in another thirty.
Matthew 13:18-23 ESV

The Lord has been creating good soil in you. This journey through the waiting, although hard, has been for your good and for His glory. Do not give up. Do not grow weary, but rest in Him. You know Him better today than you did on day one. I pray that this journey would not only lead you into joy, but that it is leading you back to your first love. Though the days seem long, they are restoring to you the joy of your salvation. Ask the Holy Spirit to finish the work He's started in your life. Rest in knowing that your waiting is not vain. You will be brought out in joy. You will experience everything your heart desires. Adjust your eyes as you refocus them on Jesus. He is the joy set before you.

Day Thirty-Three
Use What You Have

When the vessels were full, she said to her son, '
Bring me another vessel.' And he said to her, 'There
is not another.' Then the oil stopped flowing.
2 Kings 4:6 ESV

Living in the jungle meant saying goodbye to all
the comforts of home. Before we left home, I had walked
through a season of health and wellness after a long
battle with parasites that I had contracted on a previous
short term mission trip. I had worked so hard to
improve my immune system. I had all my special
vitamins and chemical free products. I was finally
healthy after a long couple years of sickness. I knew
what my body could handle and what it couldn't. Then
we walk into our waiting. We were stuck in a little
village without a postal service. There weren't many
choices when it came to vitamins and personal care
products. So, every time one of us had to leave to renew
our visas, we would stock up on everything under the
sun. All the special soaps, vitamins and essential oils.
Suitcase after suitcase we would stuff to the max. Then
as the visa runs became fewer and farther between, I
would find myself measuring out and calculating how

far we needed to stretch what we had so that we would never run out.

Soon, product after product and comfort after comfort started to run out. I was terrified of losing more comforts of home. It may seem silly, because of course they are just things, yet in the moment those products were what I knew. They were the only things that made me feel like I had some normalcy in my life. For some of these things, I would even stop using them and leave just a little bit at the bottom just in case I would really need it one day. One day I clearly heard the Holy Spirit. In His ever so calm peaceful way, I felt in my spirit, "Use what you have." I was scared to use what I had, because I knew that it would leave me empty. I was scared of empty. A season of disappointment after disappointment left me scrambling to feel full. Scrambling so much so that I was trying to fill my emptiness with something other than Jesus. I was trying to create a normal that no longer existed. I was trying to hold on to things that made me feel like the me I once knew. But there, years into my waiting I still found myself empty.

This empty was different. My life was fuller. I was experiencing joy and freedom in ways I had only dreamt of before the wilderness. I was overflowing in many ways, but I couldn't figure out why the Lord would allow me to be empty once more. Then as I walked in obedience and just used what I had, I would stand back and watch as He performed miracle after miracle even in my waiting. As I stepped out in faith and used what He had placed in my hands, I watched Him increase and multiply what we had. It's like the widow in 2 Kings 4:1-7. She needed a miracle, but all she had was a little bit of oil. So, Elisha told her to collect all the empty jars from her neighbors and as she poured, the oil multiplied over and over again until there were no more containers to fill. She was told to use what she already had in her hands. It would have been easy for her to say no, out of fear. There's no way she wanted to be empty, but in faith she used all that she had. She believed God would do the miraculous. What did the Lord do with her faith? He multiplied the oil until there was no more room. He filled her empty jugs leaving her with more than enough.

We think using what we have leaves us empty, but in the Kingdom using what we have opens the door for Jesus to multiply what He's placed in our hands. If we're not empty, then we have no use for a miracle. If we fill every spot of our lives with our own solutions, we have no use for a miracle. If you've been waiting on the Lord, there is a good chance you have felt pretty empty at times. Things haven't gone your way. Your heart is longing for the miracle you've prayed for. But it's in the empty that God does the miraculous. John 20:1-10 tells us that the tomb of Jesus was empty! It was out of that empty tomb that the greatest miracle was performed. Jesus had risen! He is alive!

God is still the miracle maker. It's who He is. All along this journey, He has placed things in your hands. It may not look like much, but He will use your faith to multiply it into the most beautiful miracles. My fear of running out of my favorite things was not an issue of not having things. It was my fear of being empty. After this intense process of waiting on the Lord I was scared to feel disappointment once again, but God, in His loving kindness, spoke directly to my heart to use what I have and to not fear the empty. He is the God of the impossible. He can create something out of nothing. He can fill and restore. He can heal and multiply. What has He placed in your hands today? What feels empty in your life that can actually be the beginning of a miracle? Could it be that God is asking you to give Him those empty thing so that He can multiply them? He's bringing increase to your life. Make room. You are in the miracle zone. He will not leave you empty. Today I pray that you see a miracle. I pray that you would see and experience the amazing love of Jesus as He makes all things new in your life.

Day Thirty-Four
A Wellspring of Refreshment

The grass withers, the flowers fade,
but the word of God remains forever.
Isaiah 40:8 HCSB

We all have different ideas of what being refreshed looks like. Maybe it's a cold drink on a hot day. Maybe it's sitting in a hammock reading your favorite book. Maybe it's playing games or watching movies with your kids after a long week of work. Maybe it's going away to your favorite spot to do your favorite hobby. Maybe it's enjoying a delicious fancy cup of coffee. While these things bring a breath of fresh air, they refresh us for just a moment. They may be a needed break in the day or the week, but those moments of refreshment come and go. The cold drink ends, the peaceful moments flee, the kids start fighting, and the fancy coffee just leaves you with five dollars less. These moments of refreshment are so needed in the middle of our busyness, but they leave our soul longing for more. Have you ever thought or said to yourself, "I'm just tired of being tired." It has become so normal in our culture to push and push ourselves leaving us to cling to these moments of refreshment that leave as quickly as they come. They help us find joy in the busy moments of life while still leaving us depleted.

We were not created to live from one moment of refreshment to the next. Our souls are looking for something that fills us, something that refreshes us and never leaves us dry. We look high and low for that thing that will make us feel less drained by the things of this world. No matter how much we think we know God, we still look outside of Him in different seasons of our lives. When we don't see Him moving or when our prayers are answered differently than we would like, we look outside of Him to seek the answers we desire. When trauma hits or the waiting begins, we do everything in our power to fix what seems to be broken to us. Could it be that it is in this place of searching where God is inviting us back to Himself? God has given us a wellspring of refreshment. God has given us Jesus. He's given us the Holy Spirit. He's given us the Bible. In Him is everything we need. In Him our hope is found. In Him we are refreshed, yet we continue searching for temporary things. We search for things that will fill the void, the stillness, the waiting.

I love sitting and enjoying a fancy cup of coffee. I love doing puzzles, reading a good book, watching a movie with my family, taking a nap, and traveling. Those things bring me joy. They refresh me. They are a needed part of my week, month, and year. They give me that breath of fresh air when the busyness of my life feels overwhelming. Those parts of my life make me feel like me, outside of being a wife, mother, daughter, and so on. The world has coined the phrase "me time" for these types of moments that bring us a moment to rest and breathe. There is nothing wrong with these moments we take for ourselves. Happy moments are never a bad thing. The problem lies when we search from one moment to the next, trying to fill our lives with temporary fixes instead of searching for the only One who can fill our souls.

I have had morning devotions for as long as I can remember. Of course, as seasons change, sometimes so would my approach to my devotions. Sometimes I would sit with Jesus in the morning and others at night. Sometimes I would have the opportunity to spend hours with Him while other times it would be a short fifteen minutes. Some seasons I would work my way through devotional books or slowly work my way through one book of the Bible at a time. I could sit in a chapter or book of the Bible for weeks and months. I always thought it was strange when I would hear someone say they were reading through the Bible in a year. I would think to myself, "Who has time for that?" "Who can actually get something out of reading through the Bible that quickly?" For so many years my devotions were part of my religious box that needed to be checked. Yes, the Holy Spirit would always do His work in me, but so many times I woke up to meet with Him only to say I did it instead of doing it to minister to His heart.

Then came my waiting. I struggled through the first few seasons as the Lord healed and restored all the places of my heart, but then I returned to my first love. I became hungry for Him once more. It was a different kind of hunger than I've felt before. I was desperate not only to be with Him, but to truly know Him. I was desperate to minister to His heart. I needed to know His Word. I needed to be able to cling to His promises. After many seasons of the Lord realigning my thinking, I needed to know who the God of the Bible actually was. Not what I had been taught or the mindsets I had formed, but who He truly is. As I hungered for Him, I started a one year reading plan. I still thought I was a little crazy for even trying it, but as I dug in and began reading through the Bible verse by verse and book by book, I found myself longing for more. I always thought it would be too much. How can I retain it all if I push myself to read the Bible from front to back? How will the Holy Spirit speak to me if I'm working through one plan for a year? But there I was every morning reading every word from front to back not feeling overwhelmed but craving more. I was craving more time to sit at His feet. I was craving to be filled with more of Him. Instead of my mindset being focused on what I could get out of my time with the Lord I began to be focused on loving Him, enjoying Him, and resting in Him. I became refreshed with Him. It was a wellspring of refreshment. Not the kind of refreshment that left me depleted from one moment to the next, but the kind that never runs dry.

When we read the Bible, we are filled with a wellspring of refreshment. We are filled with life. We are filled with Him. Isaiah 55:11 says,

"So My word that comes from My mouth will not return to Me empty, but it will accomplish what I please and will prosper in what I sent it to do." HCSB

When we spend time in God's Word, we are planting seeds in our hearts. His Word will never return void. As we are intentional to soak in every Word He's spoken, we are filled to overflowing. He will never leave us dry. What would happen if you started reading the Bible more? What would happen if you looked to Jesus for your refreshment? He will fill you. You can live in such a way that leaves you refreshed daily. I challenge you to dig into your Bible today and then spend some time journaling. Use this time to adore Him and to tell Him how much you love Him. Lay your needs and complaining down for the day and just focus on ministering to His heart. Then watch as you are washed and refreshed by His Spirit. Abundant life is yours today.

Day Thirty-Five
A Whirlwind of Hope

Then Moses stretched out his hand over the sea. The LORD drove the sea back with a powerful east wind all that night and turned the sea into dry land. So the waters were divided, and the Israelites went through the sea on dry ground, with the waters like a wall to them on their right and their left.
Exodus 14:21-22 HCSB

A whirlwind can be a lot of things. It can often times be called a tornado, a hurricane or a cyclone. It can be defined as rapid, instantaneous or sudden. In scripture we are reminded that Elijah was taken to heaven in a whirlwind and God talked to Job out of a whirlwind. When God comes in a whirlwind it's usually with His righteous anger or to bring justice. Whirlwinds often describe situations that come about swiftly that are outside of our control. We tend to view them as negative things. If we can't control the situation, that's bad, right? Whirlwinds most often bring us to our waiting. Situations outside of our control that pick us up, twirl us around, and leave us suddenly in a distant land that we don't recognize. Yet, whirlwinds can also lead us to our promise land.

Do you remember the story of Moses leading the Israelites to the Red Sea in Exodus 14? It was after Pharaoh had repeatedly refused to set them free. Egypt went through plague after plague and still, Pharaoh wouldn't let them be free. Then finally the Lord took Pharaoh's son, and he gave up. He told Moses that he would let God's people go. So as the Israelites were making their way to the Promised Land, they hit the Red Sea. They can't swim across it. They can't go around it. And of course, Pharaoh changed his mind and is now chasing them down to bring them back into slavery. Can you imagine? I imagine Moses was a little concerned as he followed God obediently only to find himself in an impossible situation. As I put myself in Moses' shoes, I can just picture the conversation I would have with God. "There's nowhere to go, we're being chased, and I know I did what you told me to do!" Can you relate?

Has your waiting led you into one impossible situation only to be surrounded by two or three more impossible situations? Walking in obedience to God, only to have door after door closed, feels like a whirlwind of disappointment. I was believing for God to part the Red Sea from the beginning. I knew He could do it, but He didn't do it when I thought He was going to. As days and months and years passed, our impossible situations just became more impossible. It caused me to question whether I had even heard the Holy Spirit at all. It caused me to doubt. It caused paralyzing fear. But do you know what it showed me? It showed me all the areas where my heart was lacking. It showed me all the areas I really didn't trust the Lord at all. The Red Sea in my waiting revealed to me all the areas that I needed more of Jesus.

The whirlwind, the chaos, turbulence and the disorder that comes quickly and leaves you without control is not always a bad thing. The whirlwind is what brings the hope.

Then Moses stretched out his hand over the sea,
and all that night the LORD drove the sea back
with a strong east wind and turned it into dry land.
The waters were divided, and the Israelites went
through the sea on dry ground, with a wall of
water on their right and on their left.
Exodus 14:21-22

The whirlwind brought the miracle. When the Lord moves, nothing is impossible. When He speaks, it is finished. When He fights for us, we walk in victory every single time. I used to be terrified of the whirlwind. Those days where it felt like we were trapped, in every direction. There was no way forward and we were being chased from behind. There were days I would question God over and over again asking Him where He was because I only saw the chaos the whirlwind was bringing.

The dangerous thing about the whirlwind is that we can be consumed by distractions. Can you imagine what would have happened if Moses was so distracted by Pharaoh chasing them that He didn't even ask the Lord what He should do? Can you imagine if Moses would have chosen fear over faith? The Israelites were terrified and thought that they were going to die. I can't imagine Moses had a quiet moment to seek the Lord while everyone was panicking in front of Him. Yet, his response to his people was,

"Do not be afraid. Stand firm and you will see the deliverance the LORD will bring you today. The Egyptians you see today you will never see again. The LORD will fight for you; you need only to be still."
Exodus 14:13-14 NIV

So often we get hit with a whirlwind and we panic. We don't seek the Lord, or we forget what He's spoken. We do everything we can to get out of the situations that we're in. We do everything in our power to get some type of order and control back. What if the whirlwind is bringing the miracle? What if God is telling us to trust Him and to walk by faith so that He can part the Red Sea in front of us? There is a whirlwind of hope that is coming to your waiting. It will happen suddenly, and you will experience the victory of the Lord. When it looks like everything is closing in on you remember that when you wait on the Lord, you will see Him move. It may not be in your timing. It may not look like you thought it would. But things will change suddenly and you will be one step closer to your promise land. Will you place your confidence in the Lord? Will you lay down every distraction that keeps you from pursuing

Him with all your heart? Will you walk by faith knowing that He does the impossible? Nothing is too hard for Him. If you are surrounded on every side and feel overwhelmed by the whirlwind swirling around you, you can rejoice, because God is fighting for you. All you have to do is be still.

Read Exodus 14 today. Be swept up in a whirlwind of hope. As things start happening in your waiting be intentional about listening to the Holy Spirit. Walk with Him. You will experience peace and freedom in new ways. Embrace this new season and worship the Lord by placing your confidence in Him alone.

Day Thirty-Six
Living Out Your Inheritance

We have also received an inheritance in Him,
predestined according to the purpose of the One who
works out everything in agreement with the decision
of His will, so that we who had already put our hope
in the Messiah might bring praise to His glory.
Ephesians 1:11 HCSB

What do you think about when you hear the word inheritance? Do you think of family heirlooms? Do you think about receiving a check that leaves you with never having to work again? Or when you hear inheritance do you roll your eyes and laugh thinking that it could never happen to you? We all have different ideas of what receiving an inheritance would look like. For so many the thought of receiving such a grand gesture seems like a far-off dream. While many won't receive a physical inheritance in this lifetime, we so often forget that we have received a spiritual inheritance! This inheritance is far greater and of far more value than any earthly inheritance could offer!

Let's take a few minutes and dive into what the Bible says about who we are. John 1:12-13 says,

"But to all who did receive Him, He gave them the right to be children of God, to those who believe in His name, who were born, not of blood, or of the will of the flesh, or of the will of man, but of God." ESV

When we receive Jesus and believe in His name, we've been given the right to be called God's children. Galatians 4:6-7 says,

"And because you are sons, God has sent the Spirit of His Son into our hearts, crying, 'Abba, Father!' So you are no longer a slave but a son, and if a son, then an heir through God." ESV

We have been adopted as sons and daughters. We've been set free from and transformed from slaves to God's children. And because we're adopted, we've been given every right as a son. We are an heir to God's kingdom! Finally, Romans 8:16-17 says,

"The Spirit Himself testifies together with our spirit that we are God's children, and if children, also heirs - heirs of God and coheirs with Christ - seeing that we suffer with Him so that we may also be glorified with Him." ESV

We are coheirs with Christ, heirs of God, children of God.

So often we forget that we have an inheritance. So often we forget who we are in Christ. The world throws curve balls at us every day and it's so easy to get sucked up into all the bad and negative things going on. So often we're tempted by the enemy to live in the hard things, forgetting who we are. Satan knows that if he can get us to forget who we are, children of God, that we will forget about our inheritance. If we forget about our inheritance, we actually forget who Jesus is and we forget who He's created us to be. The best thing about our inheritance as children of God is that it's not just for after we die. It's not something that we only receive in heaven. This inheritance has been given to us today. This inheritance can be received and utilized today as you walk through every season of life. Ephesians 1:13-14 says,

"When you heard the message of truth, the gospel of your salvation, and when you believed in Him, you were also sealed with the promised Holy Spirit. He is the down payment of our inheritance, for the redemption of the possession, to the praise of His glory." HCSB

Today, right where you are sitting, if you have received salvation through Jesus Christ, you have also received the Holy Spirit! The Holy Spirit is the down payment of our inheritance.

It says in Galatians 5:22-23 that when we receive the Holy Spirit we are filled with His fruit. Love, joy peace, patience, kindness, goodness, faithfulness, gentleness, and self-control. He is the One that we receive wisdom and knowledge from. He is the One who gives us the power to prophesy, heal the sick and cast out demons. He is the One in whom we can experience hope, freedom, joy, peace and rest. This is our inheritance. Romans 14:17 says,

"for the kingdom of God is not eating and drinking, but righteousness, peace, and joy in the Holy Spirit." HCSB

These things are ours as children of God. Because we are His, we have the Holy Spirit. Because we have the Holy Spirit, we have the ability to walk boldly and confidently in everything that the Holy Spirit has given us. This means that when trials come, we can still operate from joy. We can still have peace when the world looks like it is crashing down around us. We can still hope even when things look impossible. We can still rest when everything else points to fear, stress and worry. We can still walk in righteousness when we're tempted to walk in the ways of the world.

I have always struggled to receive things. Giving is my favorite thing in the world to do but receiving is a completely different story. As the waiting always does, it allows God to work on our heart issues. One day I was just cleaning up around the house and I clearly heard the Lord speak to my heart, "You cannot give what you have not received." It seemed random in the moment. I wasn't sitting with Him at the time or pouring my heart out in my journal. I was simply going about my day. Giving and receiving wasn't even an issue I was working through at the time, or so I thought. The Holy Spirit spoke so clearly to me though. He always sees the issues we don't see. I just went back about my day. Those words still ring loudly in my spirit, even to this day. As I sat down and processed what the Lord meant, I realized that He was addressing an issue in me that was rooted in my identity. Because I still didn't realize who I was as a child of God I wasn't able to receive the full inheritance that I had already been given.

When we really know who we are, we are able to fully possess our inheritance from the Father. We can pray for love, peace and joy, but until we know who we are and that we've been given, the Holy Spirit as our down payment, we're unable to live out our inheritance. The world around us needs the inheritance we possess, yet we cannot give until we have received. Have you received your adoption as God's child? Have you received the full inheritance that Jesus died to give you? Have you forgotten that we have not been left as orphans but have been given the Holy Spirit as your Helper. Our inheritance is for now as much as it is for when we arrive in heaven. Don't waste it or set it aside. You are blessed and highly favored. You are a son. You are a daughter. Will you live out your inheritance today? Ask the Lord what you need to do to prepare your heart to receive everything He has waiting for you. Today is the day He has made. Rejoice in it and celebrate the incredible life you've been given.

Day Thirty-Seven
Walking Out in Freedom

Therefore, if the Son sets you free, you really will be free.
John 8:36 HCSB

Freedom. When I think about freedom, I picture Jesus walking out of the tomb. Death could not hold Him. It was finished. Can you imagine how heaven was rejoicing when it was time for Jesus to resurrect? Not just rejoicing because it was Jesus, but because it marked the moment in time when God's children could experience resurrection life. Our sins had been paid for. Our debt was canceled. We're free! All because Jesus bore our sins on the cross and resurrected. There is no going back from that moment. Can you picture it?

Can you see the victory when Mary Magdalene found His tomb empty? Even after spending all that time with Jesus, Mary Magdalene and the disciples still didn't understand that Jesus would raise from the dead. They were crushed once again when they found the tomb empty. They didn't see victory. They didn't see hope. They saw confusion. They felt more grief. Even when Jesus stood in front of Mary and asked her why she was crying Mary didn't even recognize Jesus. She didn't recognize Him until He called her by name.

When we wait, we either learn to enjoy the silence and the stillness or we cave in under the pressure. I often wonder why God waited three days to resurrect Jesus. Can you imagine what the silence would have felt like between His death and resurrection? It was out of that silence that victory was declared. We have victory in every area of our lives because Jesus left the tomb. That victory leads us to freedom. Freedom to be all God created us to be. Freedom to know the voice of the Father. Freedom to live an abundant life. Freedom to choose the ways of Jesus over the ways of this world. We have been given so much freedom but so often we take it for granted. So often, we don't realize we're free.

When God asks you to wait it can oftentimes feel less like freedom and more like a prison cell. It can feel like isolation, abandonment, chaos or silence. It can feel like Daniel in the lion's den or Jonah in the whale. It can feel like Hannah praying for a baby or Joseph being sold into slavery. We don't see or feel victorious in these moments. We don't feel the freedom, yet when God calls us to wait, it ultimately brings Him glory. It also allows us to be transformed into the person He's created us to be so that we can receive the freedom and the victory that He's already given us.

When God calls us to wait it's because He's working inside of us. He's preparing us to walk in freedom. How much light can we shine in the world if we're constantly bound by things that keep us in bondage? We're not called to be slaves to the world. We're called to freedom. We're called to be sons and daughters. We're called to love the Lord with all of our heart, soul, mind and strength. We're called to love our neighbors as we love ourselves. How can we live in freedom if we're bound to the world?

I was such a people-pleaser before our days of waiting. I was also bound by fear, anxiety and worry. One day I was listening to a sermon on idols, and it was like a light bulb went off in my head. All these things that were creating this worldly part of me were actually showing me where I was putting my trust. As I started processing through the root causes of the things wrapped around my heart like fear, anxiety, worry and people-pleasing, the Holy Spirit spoke to me. I could picture Jesus chuckling over me as He said,

"If you only knew how much I loved you, you would never worry again. If you only knew how much I loved you."

This encounter with the Lord was years into my waiting. I had grown so much at this point. I had a firm foundation at this point. Yet, I still wasn't walking in freedom the way I was created to. I still struggled to put my full trust in the Lord. Even after everything He had walked me through, I still struggled to grasp His steadfast love. Then in one moment, when He spoke my name. I was free.

I won't say that I never struggle with people pleasing or I'm never tempted to worry any more, but now when those issues arise, I know how to overcome them. I remind myself that I am free. I remind myself that God has called me by name and His love for me is far greater than I can ever understand. I remind myself that Jesus paid for my freedom and my victory. I remind myself that I have a choice to either place my trust in the world or place my trust in my Father, the One who has given me abundant life. When I speak, I now speak from a place of love and a place of freedom, because I know who I am. I know who I am, because I know who He is.

The Lord has called you to wait because He is preparing you to receive His freedom. It's not a freedom of this world that can be taken away. He's given you real freedom. You may still feel tired, weary and maybe even still broken right now as you process your way through the waiting, but the Lord will not leave you feeling this way. He's working in your heart so that you can walk out of the wilderness in freedom, so when you step into your promise land you are whole, healed, and truly free. Ask the Lord to show you the blind spots in your heart. What areas are you still struggling to hold on to? What parts of your life are you still struggling to see Jesus in? Like Mary who didn't recognize Jesus at the empty tomb, are you still struggling to see Him? He's here with you right now. He's about to speak your name. Will you wait for Him? Will you trust Him? You are free to be everything that you were created to be. You are free to be you. You are free to enjoy each and every day you've been given. Your life is being restored before your eyes. Rejoice and walk in freedom! I pray that you experience the freedom that only Jesus can give. Read about the empty tomb in John 20 today. Picture the excitement, joy and freedom that heaven was experiencing when the tomb was found empty. We have that same freedom today. We're free, because Jesus lives!

Day Thirty-Eight
An Overflowing Storehouse

And when they had eat their fill, he told his disciple, 'Gather up the leftover fragments, that nothing may be lost.' So they gathered them up and filled twelve baskets with fragments from the five barley loaves left by those who had eaten.
John 6:12-13 ESV

I became so used to seeing lack along my waiting that at some point I stopped expecting to be full. I stopped asking for the miracle. I wouldn't say I stopped believing, but I was really tired of fighting day in and day out. I was still trying to do things in my own strength and on my own time. Even after years of waiting, discontentment can rear its ugly face. Yet, as the Lord works His process in our hearts as we walk through the wilderness, He begins removing the worldly desires of our hearts, replacing them with His desires.

In John 6:1-15 we read about Jesus feeding the five thousand. It's amazing to think that Jesus fed thousands of people from a little boy's offering of five loaves of bread and two fish. Not only did everyone eat until they were full, but there were twelve baskets left over! They were overflowing. I love seeing Jesus' personality in John 6:5. It says,

"Lifting up his eyes, then, and seeing that a large crowd was coming toward him, Jesus said to Philip,

'Where are we to buy bread, so that these people may eat?'" ESV

Jesus was talking to his disciple, his friend. He knew exactly what miracle was needed and that they weren't going to be buying food for five thousand people. I imagine Jesus smiling as he asked Philip this question. Jesus asked him this to test him. Would Philip see the problem or the miracle? We see this short passage of scripture happening within minutes, but can you imagine how long it would take for them to distribute food to over five thousand people? Not only did they need a miracle of multiplication, but they also needed the time to do it.

We tend to only see lack when we're hungry, when we're discontent. We tend to only see lack when problems arise, and miracles are needed. We tend to live in lack when our eyes turn away from the One who fills the storehouse. I wonder if Philip knew Jesus' heart when Jesus asked him where they were going to buy food. Did he smile with him knowing that Jesus was about to do the supernatural or did he rush into a panic trying to figure out how to fill the lack? As a friend of Jesus, how would I respond? How would you? Do we know the heart of Jesus so confidently that we prepare to watch our storehouses overflow?

There were so many days in the waiting where I felt like I would never be full again. So many days where I felt like our family would always be lacking. I even felt like I would experience lack in the Promised Land. You probably know the tired feeling I'm talking about if you've been on this journey, yet I picture the Lord in His loving kindness smiling over me and what I identify as lack. Because, in Him there is no lack. In Him is every good thing. Where I see lack, He sees a miracle. I think the Lord shows us our lack so that when we do see the overflow, we can appreciate it that much more.

Before we ever began walking through the wilderness with the Lord, a stranger had prayed a scripture over me and told me to hold on to it for the days ahead. That scripture was Philippians 4:8.

"Finally, brothers, whatever is true, whatever is honorable, whatever is just, whatever is pure, whatever is lovely, whatever is commendable, if there is any excellence, if there is anything worthy of praise, think about these things." ESV

As tiring as the lack felt, I continued to hold on to this scripture. When I was tempted to cling to the lack, I would turn my thoughts toward the good things. I would choose to be thankful. Even when it was hard and even when it hurt. And do you know what the Lord did? He began multiplying what was in our hands. It didn't happen overnight, but as my heart was molded to look more like His, my discontentment started to disappear, and my heart was satisfied. Thankfulness led us to an overflowing storehouse, just like it did when Jesus took the loaves and gave thanks. Not only were the five thousand full, but they were overflowing! If you read further in Philippians 4 Paul goes on to talk about God's provision. Verse 11-13 says,

"Not that I am speaking of being in need, for I have learned in whatever situation I am to be content. I know how to be brought low, and I know how to abound. In any and every circumstance, I have learned the secret of facing plenty and hunger, abundance, and need. I can do all things through him who strengthens me." ESV

When we confidently trust in the Miracle Maker, when we're content in all circumstances and when we give thanks, we see our lives overflow. You will not be left in lack. You will not walk out of the waiting tired, weary or hopeless. God will restore what has been lost. Not only will He restore, but He will fill your life until it's overflowing. On day one we talked about Hannah and Samuel. 1 Samuel 2:21 tells us that not only did God bless her womb with Samuel, but she also went on to have three more sons and two daughters. Overflow! What about Job? Job lost everything. Job 42:10 tells us that the Lord gave Job twice as much as he had before. Twice as much! Overflow! Think back to the lady with jars of oil. She had enough oil to pay her debts and still had enough to live on. The Bible is full of examples where God restored and gave abundantly more.

If you are feeling lack in any area, I challenge you to fix your eyes on Jesus once again. Look for the things that are lovely, honorable and true. Then praise God for what He's placed in your hands and watch as your storehouse begins to overflow. Spend time in God's word discovering His heart for you. Read through the stories we've talked about, believe, and walk by faith knowing that abundant life is yours. Overflow is happening even now. You will experience joy through life's hardest trials when your heart is satisfied in the Lord. He's been preparing your heart to receive your promise land, your miracle, your breakthrough. Be filled to overflowing so that you can pour out into the world around you. When you are filled it will overflow into your family, your friends, your job, and the world around you. Use what you've been given, give thanks, and rest confidently in the One who overflows.

Day Thirty-Nine
The Beauty of Grace Upon Grace

*For from His fullness we have all
received grace upon grace.
John 1:16 ESV*

For years I prayed to receive God in all His fullness. I wanted every part of Him. I desired Him. I longed for more of Him. I wanted to see Him move. I would sit at my piano in that spare bedroom and just ask for His fullness. I would ask for all of Him. Little did I know at the time that in order to know all of Him, or simply more of Him, I would have to walk through all different trials and testing so that I could experience Him and know His heart in all different circumstances. It's kind of like praying for patience. If you ask God to give you patience, He's most likely going to place you in situations that require you to practice patience. I wanted His fullness without the process of knowing Him through all seasons. Don't we always just want the easy way?

The Lord told me my daughter's name before we knew we were going to be walking through a long journey through the wilderness. He led me to the scripture in John 1:16 that says,

"For from His fullness we have all received grace upon grace." ESV

Her name means grace upon grace. Grace is defined as the unmerited favor of God. Some people even describe it as blessings upon blessings or favor upon favor. The thought that God wouldn't answer my prayers never even crossed my mind. There was grace and favor all over her life even before she entered this world. It's her name! How could He not come through?

Have you prayed for something and thought the same? There's no way God won't answer my prayer. It's a pray of faith. It's a prayer for the miraculous. It's a prayer that glorifies Him. Yet still, He asks us to wait. It's there, when we wait, that we discover the beauty of grace. It's in the waiting where we feel all the feelings, we make bad choices, we run or try to hide from God and yet He proves Himself true. It's in the waiting, in the silence, where we see our deepest hurts and our greatest faults. It's then that we see our need for grace. It's in that place where we truly understand what grace upon grace really is. It's easy to think that grace means we're blessed with favor and blessings. Those are the good things. Those are the things that make us feel loved or like we're on the right track in life. But what actually is grace? Grace is less about us and more about Jesus. Grace is receiving the things we don't deserve. Grace is reaping what we've never sown.

So, there we were, still waiting. Still praying. Still believing. Still walking by faith and putting one foot in front of the other. Our grace upon grace was in our arms, but the miracle we needed was nowhere to be found. As I watched her grow, I saw the favor of God on her life. I saw how beautiful and perfect she was, and I had absolutely nothing to do with it. I saw how smart and healthy she was, and I had nothing to do with it. I saw compassion and joy and love flow out of her, and I had nothing to do with it. No matter how many times I messed up, being a first-time mom, she was still exactly who God created her to be. That's the beauty of grace upon grace. I can strive to do all the right things and still fail as a parent. I can mold her the best I can and lead her to Jesus every day and still not get it all right. Because I am human. But, God. In all His fullness He has given us grace. The undeserved, unmerited favor, through His Son, Jesus.

It's through grace we have been saved. It is a gift from God. (Ephesians 2:8-9) God shows us His love in that while we were still sinners Jesus died for us. (Romans 5:8) It is not by our striving otherwise grace would not be grace. (Romans 11:6) When God says wait it's because it is in this place that we can do nothing, but rest and trust in Him. It's in the waiting where we truly see our need for grace once again. It's in the waiting where God teaches us what His grace is all about. I strived for so long in our waiting to make things happen, to push my timeline and to hang on for control. Yet, it was through the grace of God that He held us and sustained us through every moment of our wait. Where I messed up or chose worldly things, He remained faithful and true. When I ran or tried to hide, He remained constant and welcomed me home with open arms. That is grace upon grace. It's this journey of waiting where God reminds us how deeply we need Him. It's here in this place where He provides us a safe place to experience His fullness.

Grace upon grace is favor upon favor and blessings upon blessings. It might not feel like it at first, but as you look back and see all God has done in your life, I believe you will be able to testify that God was faithful, true, kind and gracious through every season of your wait. I believe you'll be able to say you have gotten a taste of His fullness and that your cup overflows. I believe that you will long for more of Him. I believe that you'll share with everyone you meet about the beauty of grace upon grace, because your time waiting on the Lord transformed you, healed you and restored you. There is so much beauty in your life today. That beauty isn't affected by the miracle you've been waiting for. The beauty you see around you is simply the grace of God in your life. Dig into your Bible today and search for scriptures on grace. Remind yourself of this precious gift that gives us the ability to experience joy through every high and every low. Praise Jesus for such a priceless gift. It's through Him we have all received grace upon grace.

Day Forty
The Promise Land

*And I heard a loud voice from the throne saying, 'Look!
God's dwelling place is now among the people, and he
will dwell with them. They will be his people, and God
himself will be with them and be their God.
Revelation 21:3 ESV*

Today is day 40. If you have been sitting at the
feet of Jesus for the last forty days, I can guarantee that
you look differently today than on day one. If you have
gone through the painful yet fruitful stages of
surrender, I imagine you are feeling peace, freedom and
joy more than you have in a long time. If you are still
struggling to embrace this season of waiting and need to
go through the forty days once more, there is no shame
in that. Start the forty days again. Keep digging in. Keep
surrendering. Keep growing. Keep pushing. You will
walk into your promise land. I would love to tell you
that once you get to day forty, all your struggles will go
away. I would love to tell you that your waiting is over,
your miracle has arrived, your breakthrough is here.
But the truth is, I don't know where you are in your

season of waiting on the Lord. I don't know when your miracle will manifest or when you will physically experience the promise land you've been picturing. Here is what I do know....

God knew your name before you were born. He made you in His image. He has called you His daughter, His son. You were born into sin. But, Jesus. God sent His One and only Son to be born of a virgin and to die a horrific death on a cross to save you from an eternal separation from the Father. After three days He resurrected and then ascended to heaven so that He could be seated at the right hand of God. His blood was shed for you and for me. His body was broken for you and for me. It's Jesus. Jesus is our promise land. Jesus is everything we need. He's everything we could ever dream about or desire. God gave us everything through the sacrifice of His Son. Jesus gave us everything by laying His life down for us so that we could live. He's our goal. He's our reward. He's the reason we live. It's all about Jesus.

A promise land can be described as a happy place. The ultimate goal in life. A place where all our hopes and dreams come true. Picture your promise land. What is it that your heart has been longing for? Why has the Lord brought you on this journey of waiting? Is it joy that you've been after? Our joy is found in Jesus. Is it peace? Our peace is found in Jesus. Is it a healthy family? Jesus is our healer. Everything that we could ever desire is found in Him. He's our promise land. He's the reason we're alive. He's the reason we have hope. He's the reason we are able to rejoice every single day, because we are fully known and fully loved by the One that gave it all so that we can have eternal life. He's the reason we're able to possess the promises of God. Jesus is the only One that can fill every void we feel. He's the only one that satisfies.

God does miracles. It's what He does. We don't have to beg Him to do them. It's just who He is. He's not moved by our worry or fear. He's not shaken when life's not going the way we've planned. Our confidence is in who He is, not what He does or doesn't do. If the Lord has asked you to wait on Him, it's because it's part of His plan. He knows what you think you're waiting on. He also knows the incredible things that He has waiting for you. Will you trust Him? Will you continue to seek Him, love Him, and worship Him when you don't understand?

I pray that you have received a revelation of Jesus through these last forty days. I pray that you know the faithful, steadfast love of the Lord. I pray that you have experienced His kindness and goodness as I have, walking through the waiting. I pray that you can testify to His grace and mercy. I pray that the words in this book have helped you fall more in love with Him. I pray that you are healed, whole and free to be all that God created you to be. I pray that you continue growing and maturing in His love. I pray that, if you are still waiting on the Lord, you would be encouraged and filled with hope knowing that you are loved, held and that He is doing an incredible work in you. If your miracle has arrived, I celebrate with you and pray that you would remember this journey of waiting every day for the rest of your life. Remember who Jesus is in every season. Praise Him and worship Him through the mountaintops and the valleys. I pray above all that Jesus has been glorified in your journey.

Thank you for walking through the waiting with me. I pray that you met Jesus in every page. Our victory has been won. Our promise land is secured. I hope you've found the joy that I have along this journey through the wilderness. May you experience abundant life in every way. May you be filled to overflowing. May your joy be found when God says wait.

Made in the USA
Coppell, TX
20 September 2021

62697224R00115